KICKING THE DRUG HABIT

ABOUT THE AUTHOR

Michael Anthony Corey was born in Charleston, West Virginia in 1957. A summa cum laude graduate in Developmental Psychology, Michael earned a nontraditional doctorate in the Psychology of Religion in 1985. His educational background is unusually diverse, having been trained in both medicine and the physical sciences as well as in philosophy and the psychology of religion.

His dissertation was based on a series of pioneering discoveries which he made regarding the nature of human identity formation and the various psychological mechanisms surrounding character development. He has since devoted his life to the creation of an exciting new theology based on a full-scale integration of Jungian depth psychology and traditional Christian theology, which he is convinced will shed new light on the age-old problem of human evil.

A frequent contributor to professional academic journals, Michael has been actively involved in the development of new treatment modalities for drunk driving offenders. He has written on such topics as the nature of self-fulfilling prophecy, the psychology of channeling, feminist politics, the nature and treatment of addiction, the integration of evolutionism and creationism, the existence of God, and the philosophical themes underlying many of today's most popular movies.

A staunch environmentalist and proponent of nutritional medicine, Michael also enjoys traveling, jogging, and listening to jazz. In 1988 he served as the executive producer for a high-tech jazz-fusion album, on which he also played the guitar.

KICKING THE DRUG HABIT

A Comprehensive Self-Help Guide
to Understanding the Drug Problem
and Overcoming Addiction

By

MICHAEL ANTHONY COREY

CHARLES C THOMAS • **PUBLISHER**
Springfield • Illinois • U.S.A.

Published and Distributed Throughout the World by

CHARLES C THOMAS • PUBLISHER
2600 South First Street
Springfield, Illinois 62794-9265

©*1989 by* MICHAEL ANTHONY COREY

ISBN 0-398-05608-0

Library of Congress Catalog Card Number: 89-4625

With THOMAS BOOKS *careful attention is given to all details of manufacturing
and design. It is the Publisher's desire to present books that are satisfactory as to their
physical qualities and artistic possibilities and appropriate for their particular use.*
THOMAS BOOKS *will be true to those laws of quality that assure a good name
and good will.*

Printed in the United States of America
SC-R-3

Library of Congress Cataloging-in-Publication Data

Corey, Michael A.
    Kicking the drug habit : a comprehensive self-help guide to
understanding the drug problem and overcoming addiction / by Michael
A. Corey.
      p.   cm.
    Bibliography: p.
    Includes index.
    ISBN 0-398-05608-0
    1. Drug abuse. I. Title.
    RC564.C684 1989
    362.29—dc20   89-4625
                                                           CIP

To Nahia and Beth

Dedicated to the Memory of Paul Leslie Lewis

ACKNOWLEDGMENTS

There are several people I would like to thank for their help and inspiration during the writing of this book.

First and foremost, I would like to thank my parents, who have stood behind me all the way. Without them, this book would never have been possible.

I would also like to thank Nahia, who was undoubtedly the most critical component in the genesis of this manuscript. She believed in the reality of this book a full ten years before it was ever written, and it was this belief which single-handedly enabled it to come to fruition. Many thanks also to Beth, for being such great company over the years.

In addition, I would like to thank my brother Johnny for helping to inspire several portions of this manuscript. If his tremendous sincerity and boundless enthusiasm could be effectively harnessed, all the world's problems would be instantly solved! I would also like to thank Danny, my brother and expert legal counsel, for his help and encouragement during this entire project.

I am also grateful to my cousin Steve, for his brilliant advice and encouragement when I needed it most, as well as to Marta and her family for being so kind to me throughout my ordeal. I would also like to thank Father Olof Scott for his timely advice and super sermons, along with all the great Sunday School kids I've taught over the years.

Many thanks also go out to Greg, Elliot, Sammy, Chuck, Abu, Mr. Hyde, and all my other friends who have helped to inspire my thoughts over the years.

Thanks also to Liz, JK, Janice, Kris, Adele, Marvin, Jane, Denis, Kathy, Lecia, Nina, Julie, Francisco, and Mina for their kindness and thoughtfulness whenever I'm on the West Coast.

Finally, I would like to thank the following musicians for inspiring me on a daily basis: Jeff Lorber, Chick Corea and his phenomenal Elektric Band, Richard Elliot, Larry Carlton, David Sanborn, Hidden Agenda,

The Wave, Slow Burn, Fattburger, Juan Carlos Quintero, and the Yellowjackets. Many thanks also to RZ Studios for their great jazz.

Last but not least, I would like to thank the great Creator of the Universe, because it is His Belief in our future potential which makes all our struggling worthwhile in the end.

CONTENTS

KICKING THE DRUG HABIT

WARNING

DRUG ADDICTION IS A SERIOUS MEDICAL PROBLEM WHICH CAN CAUSE DEATH IF IT IS NOT HANDLED PROPERLY. CONSEQUENTLY, THIS BOOK IS ONLY MEANT TO BE AN ADJUNCT TO, AND NOT A SUBSTITUTE FOR, EXPERT MEDICAL TREATMENT.

Chapter 1

INTRODUCTION

I am a recovered drug abuser. Although I was never a bona fide addict in the sense of taking strong addicting drugs like heroin or cocaine every day, for a period of about two years in high school I habitually consumed just about every psychoactive drug that I could get my hands on. My drug of choice was high-grade marijuana, but I also took LSD, PCP, Quaaludes, Percodans, amphetamines, barbiturates, and occasionally a little cocaine.

At the time I really loved my daily habit of illicit drug use. It was literally the most important thing in my entire life back then. Somehow I managed to keep a straight "A" average in school, but drugs were always the main focus of my day-to-day activities.

But it wasn't as if I was alone in my drug-using habit. On the contrary, virtually every single one of my close friends were into using drugs just as much as I was. In fact, only two of my friends were clear non-users, and that was only because they had already been through the whole drug-using phase of adolescence and had gotten over it.

It's hard for non-drug users to understand how drugs can become the absolute focus of one's life, but it really does happen all too easily, especially when you're a teenager. Once you learn that ecstasy can be repeatedly obtained with just the right combination of drugs, every other experience literally pales in comparison. This phenomenon can even be seen in the laboratory. If rats are given the choice between cocaine and food, they will choose cocaine repeatedly until they actually die from starvation.

So when I say that I loved using drugs more than anything else in my whole life, I really mean it. Little did I realize that my overwhelming pleasure would soon turn into unbelievable pain and suffering.

My parents had repeatedly warned me about the dangers of drug abuse, but I didn't believe them. How could I? All that I had ever felt on drugs was great; virtually all of my friends were also into drugs, and anyway, how could they possibly expect me to listen to

3

them when virtually their entire generation drank alcohol and smoked cigarettes?

On the contrary, everytime they insisted that I give up drugs I wanted to do them all the more, just to spite them. It was a very bad situation to be sure, but it was only the beginning of the horrors that I was about to experience.

This book is about the many perils of drug abuse. It has five major goals:

1. To explain our society's current obsession with drugs.
2. To describe the effects and hazards of the most commonly abused drugs.
3. To show what can go wrong with one's body and mind when one continues to abuse drugs.
4. To show how one can kick the drug habit forever, no matter how deeply one is into it.
5. To show how we as a nation can best deal with the drug problem.

However, this book will be considerably different from virtually all the others on this subject, since it is written, not from the perspective of a sterile, uninvolved clinician, but rather from the perspective of someone who has been there and who has been lucky enough to survive. Hopefully, this kind of direct experience will make the book far more relevant to the drug abuser and his family than a cold, disconnected literary treatise on the subject ever could be.

The course of the book will be as follows: In the next chapter the hair-raising saga of my own personal nightmare with drugs will be described in detail. We will then go on to describe the current dimensions of the drug problem, both in this country and around the world. From there we will go on to consider one of the most provocative topics on the subject of drug abuse: why people actually use drugs in the first place. This will be followed by a chapter which catalogs both the effects and the hazards of the most popular types of psychoactive drugs. Then, once the problem has been sufficiently described, we will go on to show how the addict can kick his drug habit forever using a variety of powerful health-building techniques. Finally, we will discuss what both society and the family can do to help reduce the incidence of drug abuse in the general population.

This book is written both for the drug abuser himself and his family. It will be most helpful to the abuser who has already made a conscious decision to kick the drug habit, but it can also be used to advantage by both confirmed drug addicts and their families. Indeed, families of addicts need almost as much practical information about drug abuse as addicts themselves do, since they are usually so intimately involved with the problem and, hence, need a reliable source of information before they can take the appropriate action. It is my sincere hope that this book will provide both addicts and their families with all the help they need in order to be able to solve their drug problems once and for all.

Chapter 2

A BRUSH WITH DEATH

As I mentioned in the Introduction, for the two-and-a-half years or so that I engaged in drug abuse, I couldn't have had a better time. I absolutely loved getting high. Music sounded better, food tasted better, and best of all, everything always seemed right with the world when I had a "buzz.", Indeed, I found this sense of global optimism particularly reassuring, since I was hyper-aware of all the problems that our poor world was experiencing back in the mid-seventies.

I also played in a rock band at the time, and drugs naturally fit into my ultra-hip life-style. I was convinced that getting high enhanced my musical creativity, but even if it didn't, it at least made the music sound better.

Better yet was how dope made me feel. I honestly felt TERRIFIC when I was high, and nothing else could even come close to duplicating this system-wide euphoric feeling. All negative emotions would instantly disappear as soon as I would do a "bong hit" or two; they would be replaced by a sense of joy and hilarity that simply could not be equaled by any other experience in life. Even my physical body felt better when I was high.

Most of all, my drug use allowed me to fit into the "right" crowd. Just about everyone my age got high back in the mid-seventies, so in order to be "cool," one simply had to go with the flow and get high as well. However, most people were able to control their drug use; their bodies and minds were able to adapt to the extreme physiological stress induced by drugs, but I was different. I was intrinsically much more sensitive to the effects of these chemicals, and it was because of this extraordinary sensitivity that I was about to be catapulted into one of the worst nightmares imaginable.

Frighteningly enough, at the time, I didn't have a clue that my drug use would eventually get me into health trouble. All my problems happened literally overnight; indeed, the day before all this trouble developed, I had one of the best highs of my life!

6

Amazingly, I went through my first ten years of public school as straight as an arrow. My Christian upbringing and extremely creative childhood made the very thought of drugs seem like a joke. Life was far too much fun to even think about ruining it all by getting high. Significantly enough, though, almost none of my other friends had started getting high yet either.

Then it happened. I went to an Emerson, Lake, and Palmer concert towards the end of my sophomore year in high school and finally succumbed. The group I was sitting with started getting high, and since a couple of my very best friends were smoking, the urge to get high was literally overwhelming.

At first I resisted. After all, how could I let down God, my wonderful parents, and the pursuit of right? How could I allow myself to become a "sleazy" drug abuser? I didn't want to become addicted. I had far too much to lose—a perfect academic record of straight "A's," a happy home life, and a promising future in college.

On the other hand, though, the people I was with didn't look like sleazy drug addicts at all. On the contrary, they were some of the most attractive and popular people in our entire city. They didn't act like psychotic drug fiends either; instead, they seemed to be having the time of their lives.

Then it dawned on me. I had been lied to all those years by my parents and the rest of society: drug use wasn't the overly outrageous evil that they said it was; it was by far the most enjoyable thing that one could possibly do in life. That's why they said it was so bad: not because it really was so bad, but because it was so good. They knew that once I tried it, I would like it forever, so they did their best to keep me from ever trying it in the first place. In short, they grossly exaggerated the evils of drug use just to keep me from using them.

In retrospect, I realize that it was at the concert that I lost my childhood innocence—not simply because I started smoking pot but because I had reached the end of the first major stage of my pre-adult existence. For instead of just taking the establishment's word for things, as I had done my entire life up until then, I suddenly felt the need to start finding things out for myself. In short, I suddenly found myself immersed in the rebelliousness which is so characteristic of adolescence.

In other words, it wasn't the marijuana per se which made me so rebellious, it was my rebelliousness which made me start smoking pot and using other drugs. Thus, in a very real sense drug abuse among teens appears to be more a consequence of growing up than anything else.

According to the Bible, Adam and Eve went through a similar period of rebelliousness. Even though God clearly told them not to eat from the Forbidden Tree, they couldn't resist. They couldn't just take God's Word for it—they had to find out for themselves.

In the same way, I couldn't just blindly take my parents' word for it that drugs were so evil, especially when they seemed like so much fun. I had to find out for myself. But just as Adam and Eve's transgression caused them more grief than they could have ever imagined at the time, my own personal transgression also led me into more suffering than I ever knew was even possible.

Surprisingly enough, I didn't get high at the concert, even though I smoked a good amount. I didn't know that it sometimes takes a good while before one is able to get high from smoking pot.[1] However, I was able to get high on my very next attempt, and my deepest suspicions were finally validated: smoking pot wasn't evil after all, it was fun! Now I knew why everyone had made such a big deal over smoking pot—because it was so great that it made everything else literally pale in comparison!

This explained why society was dead set against the smoking of pot. Since pot smoking was so intensely pleasurable, there was no way that any of the rewards of the straight society could ever possibly compete with the internal rewards of getting high. Thus, the "square" establishment was simply jealous of the pleasure that pot was able to deliver, so in order to keep as many people as possible away from the enemy camp, it naturally chose to oppose the use of marijuana with every power at its disposal.

I simply loved having my state of consciousness changed by the mere smoking of some weed. Everything suddenly became so much more interesting and fun. I now realize that I had been terrifically bored at the time; pot enabled me to escape my boredom with the simple lighting of a joint. (This is a major reason why so many young people are resorting to drug use these days—because they are literally bored sick with their lives. We simply are not providing them with enough interesting activities both in and out of school, so they turn to drug use to escape their boredom.)

My immediate fascination with marijuana only intensified my dissatis-

---

1. The marijuana which was available back in the mid-seventies was an average of ten times weaker than it is today. This is undoubtedly why it took so long back then for a person to get high for the first time.

faction with my parents. Not only had they lied to me about the most important thing in the world, they did it with such passion and downright hostility that I could have puked. How could I possibly approve of them when they were so concerned about ruining my life with their ridiculous rules? I was doing fine in school, so what right did they have of trying to run my life according to their own game plan? Babies don't like it when you try to take a sucker out of their mouths, and teens don't like it when their parents try to take the only pleasure in their lives away from them.

Literally overnight, my parents, along with the rest of society, became my cumulative enemy. After all, the smoking of pot was just one aspect of my own inner process of psychological development, so by opposing my use of pot, I figured that they were also opposed to my growing up. This of course made me angry. But since I was still so dependent on them, I couldn't afford to antagonize them too much, so I took it upon myself to hide my drug use from them as much as possible. I used Visine and a couple of Certs after every joint, and hid my pot in the most creative of places.

But in spite of all that, I still couldn't hide my drug use from my parents for very long. They could tell from my behavior that I was getting high, even though I tried like the dickens to "be cool" with my behavior. (However, I eventually did perfect the art of behaving normally, in spite of being totally wasted on the inside.) This of course only intensified the friction in our home, and when my younger brother started smoking pot, things really began to get bad.

In a typically adolescent fashion, I interpreted my parents' extremely vocal reprimands as being Anti-Me, so I responded by using even more drugs. This of course is called spite and it is undoubtedly one of the most profoundly destructive things in the entire world! It was certainly one of the biggest reasons why I continued to smoke pot, even when it became obvious that things were rapidly getting out of control in my life. Indeed, if my parents had told me not to jump off a bridge at the time, I would have been tempted to go ahead and do it anyway, just because of my overwhelming urge to spite them![2]

Almost immediately after I started smoking pot, my entire life began to change radically. I suddenly took on a much more "hip" appearance;

---

2. For a detailed psychological analysis of the nature of spite in teens, please refer to the discussion on spite in Chapter 4.

my hair got longer and my clothes got funkier. In order to devote as much time as possible to my new obsession, I dropped out of our school band and quit playing on our church basketball team. Although soon thereafter I helped to start a surprisingly successful rock band, my life still continued to shrink away from that of the traditional straight society.

This was undoubtedly the most outrageously enjoyable year that I had ever had in my entire life! My band was playing at school and church functions, my friends and I were having a blast every single day getting high, my grades were perfect, and I felt great. Indeed, that was the only year that I ever went without having a single cold or major viral illness.

But just as surely as my junior year was so great, my senior year suddenly took on a much more reflective and ominous tone. Out of nowhere I began to get seriously depressed for the first time in my life. All of a sudden, instead of enjoying myself whenever I would get high, I would become quiet and introspective. And needless to say, when a teenager starts to look deep inside his own psyche, he's bound to get depressed sooner or later.

My depression and drug toxicity began to show itself in class. Although I still made straight A's, it was becoming harder and harder to do so. My mind would wander excessively during class, and during tests it would often go totally blank. Fortunately for me, I was lucky enough to have some of the most helpful and understanding teachers in the entire world, who repeatedly went far out of their way to help me out during school. They knew I was into drugs, but instead of condemning me for it, they chose to elicit my cooperation through their compassionate understanding. I will always love them for that.

My relationships with my friends also began to suffer around this time. I had become such a jerk that even my best friend began to give me the shake. Most distressingly, my straight girlfriend began to get too overwhelmed by my heavy thinking and excessive morbidity, and for good reason: when I was with her I would concentrate solely on the very worst things in life and stay up into the wee hours of the morning telling her about them. After awhile, she became totally fed up and proceeded to break up with me. This of course only intensified my depression, as did each successive time I smoked pot.

However, all this was a mere trifle compared to the nightmare I was soon to experience. Even at this point, though, I had absolutely no idea of what was about to happen to me.

My serious problems began a few weeks after my high school graduation, when I decided to attend a church convention in Cleveland with several of my friends. I had just scored several hits of LSD and some killer weed, and I was determined to have the best high of my entire life.

After distributing the LSD amongst my friends, I proceeded to rent a room all by myself so that I could have the most mystical experience that was humanly possible: I didn't just want to see colors—I wanted to see God Himself.

I now realize that I was actually trying to reach a very laudable goal with my strategic LSD use—psychological maturity, along with the spiritual insight and understanding which naturally come with it. Unfortunately, I didn't realize at the time that this type of maturity simply cannot be obtained through drugs, no matter how heroically one tries; it can only be gradually obtained through suffering and hard work. Ironically, though, my drug use indirectly helped me to attain my goal by causing me to suffer and struggle horrendously for years, because suffering and struggling are the very things that help to generate psychospiritual maturity in people.

Once I entered my room, I proceeded to take around 40 or so bong hits of my killer weed. That *really* got me wasted—so wasted in fact that I had to sleep it off. But like a lunatic I swallowed a hit of LSD before I dozed off, because when I'm determined to do something as grandiose as meeting God, I will do everything imaginable to attain my goal. Unfortunately, I didn't realize that there was someone else I could just as easily end up meeting. . . .

Well, after sleeping for about an hour I began to have the most horrendous nightmare of my life. Mere words could never begin to describe how terrifying it was. In fact, it soon became so totally frightening that I did the customary thing under the circumstances—I woke up. But since my nightmare was due to the LSD that I had just taken, it didn't go away when I awakened. On the contrary, it got twice as bad just as soon as I opened my eyes. And as if that weren't enough, it proceeded to get progressively worse and worse as time went on, so that by late that night I was in a total unabashed panic. (Although it's hard for anyone who's never had a bad trip on LSD to imagine what it must be like, the very thought of having an actual nightmare persist throughout the waking day begins to describe the experience.)

I was totally out of my mind at the time. All of the former rules and queues for conscious functioning that I had learned throughout my life suddenly became totally meaningless. Trillions of fragmented thoughts of impending doom suddenly began to pound my conscious mind all at the same time. My whole body was shaking and rushing from the speed in the acid; I didn't know who I was or where I was. It was as if my entire life had suddenly short-circuited before my very eyes. It was so horrible that mere words will never adequately describe the experience.

But that wasn't all. Within a few terrifying minutes of being awake, I suddenly began to feel an ominous presence in the room. Although it was undoubtedly the result of a profound LSD-induced change in my state of mind, I subjectively experienced the event as meeting the devil himself—and it literally scared me to death!

Because it's impossible to fully describe this indescribable experience, the best that I can do is to say that this evil presence began to badger me with what seemed like an endless stream of hostile and evil accusations. It was sheer psychological torture, worse than anything else that I'd ever imagined up until then. This went on for some time and was so intolerable that if I could have killed myself at the time I probably would have done so. In retrospect, I realize that my current belief in the reality of hell began precisely at that moment. I believe in hell because I've actually been in hell.

Even worse was how my conscious mind felt at the time. It was as if I had been poisoned to death, but for some reason was being forced to survive the poisoning just so I could feel what it was like. It was the most grotesque and nauseating physiological experience imaginable.

It was like being on a huge roller coaster where you are just trying to hang on for dear life so that you won't fly out and splatter on the ground. I wanted to cry in response to all the formerly repressed pains which were suddenly being released in my conscious mind, but I never really got the chance. For every time a discrete emotional pain from my past would enter my conscious experience, it would suddenly be followed by a completely different pain, which in turn would be followed by another and still another. LSD thus fragmented my mind to the point that I could only experience bits and pieces of my true feelings. Consequently, I could never cry in response to any one feeling because I could never "catch up" to it—just as soon as it would come it would go, only to be followed by another fleeting feeling.

Needless to say, my emotional state was greatly affected by the fact that so many different emotions were suddenly presenting themselves to me at the same time. We are all used to feeling one thing at a time or possibly two or three—but not hundreds of different things all at once! It was like being constantly buffeted by an emotional whirlwind. I couldn't feel any one thing for very long because I was getting constantly badgered by so many different things. All I could do was to try to hang on in order to keep from getting literally blown away by the whole experience.

This lack of mental control over my own inner experiences was totally horrifying. We are all used to having a large degree of control over our own thoughts and feelings; indeed, the very definition of the word sanity assumes a certain amount of this control. But what happens when a deliberately ingested chemical causes you to lose total control over your own mind?[3] You temporarily go mad, and there is absolutely nothing in the entire repertoire of human experience which is as frightening and unnerving, because at the time there is absolutely nothing you can do on your own to stop the experience, short of suicide. (There are effective medical antidotes for LSD overdoses—such as Thorazine and Haldol—but you need to be seen by a doctor in order to get them. However, this is rather unlikely when you are in the throes of a bad LSD trip.)

After a few hours of this constant inner buffeting, I finally got up enough courage to go downstairs to see my friends. As soon as I stepped outside my room I felt far too conspicuous and paranoid to continue, but I forced myself to go ahead anyway, because I knew that I couldn't tolerate another moment of this profound suffering alone.

Unfortunately, though, my ongoing nightmare didn't go away when I saw my friends. On the contrary, it got much worse, because the very sight of them totally freaked my mind out. It was horrible. When they began to badger each other in fun-loving jest, I started to shake from the excruciating pain it caused me, because what was fun for them was devilishly painful torture for me. Nevertheless, I succeeded in putting up with it all, because I really didn't have any other choice in the matter apart from outright suicide.

It was then that I began to realize why some people actually kill themselves while on drugs. The experience can be so intolerably horrible that seemingly the only way out is suicide. Still, suicide was not the

---

3. Most of my temporary loss of mental control was undoubtedly caused by an LSD-induced failure of the repressive process in my brain. Absolutely nothing short of hell is as terrifying as a sudden loss in the mind's ability to repress pain. Indeed, in my own psychologically based theology this is exactly what hell is: a complete and total loss in the ability to repress unconscious pain. This is reason alone for a person to never do drugs again: because you never know when a given drug will cause a total failure in the mind's repressive process.

"solution" I wanted, so I decided to do my best to wait until I could "come down" from the evil drug effects, because then I would hopefully be able to recapture my sanity again. (Had I known that there was an effective medical antidote for my LSD poisoning, I would have gone straight to the emergency room.)

One way or another I ended up going to a Shakespearean play that night with two of the most humorous and bizarre people that I knew. Unfortunately, though, what is humorous while one is straight is sheer psychological torture when one is out of one's mind on LSD. They will never know how much they tortured me on the way to the play with their radically humorous comments about the city and people of Cleveland. Even the play itself freaked me out, what with its bizarre costumes and lines and all.

To my credit, though, I endured the entire nightmarish experience and finally got to sleep late that night. When I woke up a few hours later I was overjoyed to find that the nightmare was finally over, although I still felt the toxic effect of the drug in my mind. I also felt extremely shaky, both mentally and physically, so I didn't even consider smoking pot the rest of the day. This was the first time in my life that I ever realized how utterly priceless psychological normality is and how, when it goes, it takes nothing less than a totally heroic effort to get it back again.

Despite my hellish experience, I started smoking pot again the very next day, and although my highs were quite uneventful, I could tell that my inner mind was still extremely shaky from my once-in-a-lifetime experience. You'd think that such a living nightmare would have been enough to get me to quit drugs forever, but such a naive assumption underestimates how profoundly addicting drugs can be—even such a "safe" and "non-addicting" drug as marijuana.[4] So when I say that drugs were my entire life back then, I mean it! It would have been easier for me to lose a finger or even an entire limb than to give up my drug habit.

Then it happened. I went away to school with the rest of my buddies, and soon thereafter my whole life began to fall apart. It wasn't gradual either, at least not as far as I could tell. Somehow I felt vaguely uneasy as I attended my first few classes, and then, BOOM, it happened. Something in my brain "clicked" as I was walking into the university bookstore

---

4. Marijuana is only non-addicting from a physiological standpoint, and even then it is still addicting to some extent, since upon abrupt cessation of use it usually elicits some sort of negative withdrawal symptoms. Psychologically speaking, though, ALL psychoactive drugs are profoundly addicting, *especially* marijuana and cocaine.

one day, and then all of a sudden, I began to have the most distressing and uncomfortable feeling imaginable in the back of my head. It wasn't just a routine psychological disturbance, as my extremely shortsighted doctor originally suggested. It was an actual physiological sensation somewhat akin to a drug effect which was utterly intolerable for me.

There was nothing I could do to shake that maddening occipital pain. But while I couldn't make it better, I could easily make it much worse by smoking pot or by consuming any type of psychoactive drug. Even so, do you think I was able to quit smoking pot at that point? No way! I was hooked to the daily ritual much too strongly to be able to quit so easily, even though it made me feel worse every time I got high. I suppose I was just hoping that my bad reactions would instantly vanish one day so I could be just like everybody else, but they never did. Instead, they got worse.

In retrospect, my inner deterioration was the result of three interrelated factors:

1. The initial traumatizing of my psychological defenses from the bad acid trip a few months earlier.
2. The inherent stress of moving away to school and starting the stressful life of a college student trying to make straight A's.
3. The accumulated toxicity of all the high-grade marijuana and hashish that I had continued to smoke.

Once I discovered that this agonizing feeling in the back of my head wasn't going to go away, I went to see a psychiatrist at the Student Health Center. This was the biggest mistake that I could possibly have ever made, for while we may have had a few beneficial chats from time to time, the doctor unknowingly began to seal my fate forever by prescribing a major tranquilizer and a potent antidepressant for me.

What neither I nor my doctor realized at the time was that the vast majority of my problem was my inordinate hypersensitivity to all the drugs I was taking. You don't solve a toxicity problem by prescribing even more toxic chemicals, but that is exactly what the doctor did.

I proceeded to get worse and worse with each passing day, and there was nothing I could do to make the problem any better. As usual, though, there was something I could do to make it worse, and I did: I started smoking cigarettes. I didn't realize it at the time, but I am extremely allergic to cigarette smoke, so by starting to smoke I was unknowingly hammering the last nail in my own hypertoxicity coffin.

My brain proceeded to react in characteristic fashion to all the poisonous chemicals that were repeatedly raping it. It got more and more inflamed and painful with each passing day, so that all I could do was hang desperately on until a solution could hopefully be found.

Incredibly enough, my performance in school was still admirable, even though my neurological status was being increasingly compromised with each additional tranquilizer I took. I made three A's and one B in my four classes, and I was one of the very few A's in our exceedingly difficult biology class. (It was so difficult in fact that our class succeeded in filing a complaint against the biology department.)

As the semester wore on, I found that my reactions to getting high were progressively getting worse and worse. But marijuana had become such an integral part of my life that I couldn't even imagine giving it up—so I continued to smoke every day, even though it made me feel so darned bad. In the process I only made myself worse and worse.

I guess I kept hoping that one day I would wake up and everything would suddenly be back to normal again. After all, when you see your very best friends getting high with absolutely no ill effects, it is disconcerting and even frightening to realize that for some strange reason you can't do the same thing anymore. What I didn't realize at the time was that I had built up a certain amount of biochemical "toxicity" in my brain with all the poisons that I had relentlessly been taking, so much so that I would never be back to normal until I eliminated ALL the poisons from my body once and for all.

Not having the luxury of hindsight to help guide me along, I continued to take my prescribed tranquilizers every single day, which in turn caused me to get worse and worse. You'd think that a psychiatrist who had been educated for more than half his lifetime would be aware of this problem, but mine certainly wasn't, and as far as I'm concerned, he was guilty of criminal neglect. My life was rapidly deteriorating because of all the drugs he was routinely giving me, and yet he didn't even know it! This is totally inexcusable, but the same thing happens thousands of times a day all over the world to all sorts of poor innocent victims! Psychiatry has a long way to go before it realizes what true mental health is really all about and how it can best be obtained.

As the semester drew to a close, I decided to drop out for a while, since the inner psychological discomfort I was experiencing was so intolerable. This decision was made all the more palatable since several of my other closest buddies also decided to drop out so that we could put our band back together again.

Unfortunately, once I got back home things failed to get any better at all. The Christmas of '76 in particular turned out to be a pitiful fiasco. My girl friend finally broke up with me once and for all on Christmas Eve because she couldn't deal with my problems anymore, and to top it all off, I had a very bad reaction to another round of marijuana smoking. Consequently, there wasn't much else I could do once I got home but cry myself to sleep while the world waited for Santa Claus to mysteriously drop by for a visit.

I found it almost impossible to believe that marijuana could suddenly have such a profoundly negative effect on me. After all, for two-and-a-half years I had gotten nothing but pleasure from it, so what could possibly have made things change? It was crazy. Even though pot made me feel so much worse, I still couldn't quit. It was too much a part of my life for me to quit. Marijuana smoking is one of the few behaviors which is next to impossible to extinguish without something severe happening to make you quit. Indeed, if I hadn't reacted so severely, it is extremely doubtful that I would have ever been able to quit.

The institutionalized joy of Christmas really puzzled the hell out of me—I just couldn't figure out how people could appear to be having such an outrageously good time while I found so much to be miserable about. This is undoubtedly why the suicide rate is so much higher during the holidays: because for many depressed people the contrast between their misery and everyone else's happiness is often too much to bear.

By this time I had become convinced that I was crazy, and this rapidly became a self-fulfilling prophecy for me. It all began on the last day of the semester when I had my final visit with my psychiatrist. At the end of our session he had me take my chart up to the nurse's station, but on the way I took a quick peek inside and read that I was diagnosed as a possible "schizoid personality." Not knowing that the term "schizoid personality" only refers to a reclusive sort of individual (which for me was an appropriate form of behavior at the time), I concluded that it meant that I was really and truly crazy, in the deepest and most inexorable sense of the word.

Well, as soon as I read that diagnosis I immediately lost all hope in my potential recovery. After all, here was a mental health professional with years and years of experience who was saying I was a schizoid personality, which of course I interpreted as meaning hopelessly crazy forever. That explained it! I had been suffering so badly because I was crazy! Even worse, I thought that I didn't have a chance in hell of ever snapping out of it, because everyone knows that crazy people don't ever get better![5]

This inner conviction that I was crazy only intensified the profound inner misery I was experiencing. What it did was erase all hope from my life, and that turned out to be the last blow to my already fragile personality structure.[6]

It's hard to describe how difficult it is to try to live without hope in one's life. In fact, it was so bad that just being awake was intolerable for me, so I did everything I could to sleep as much as possible. I would stay up until seven or eight in the morning and then, with the help of huge doses of tranquilizers, I would sleep all day and into the night. There for awhile I even spent the majority of three consecutive weeks glued to our couch, where I continuously brooded about the tragic fate that had happened to me.

Words can't describe how painful my inner experiences were at the time. They truly were intolerable. But what do you do when your inner psychological state is intolerable? Well, there's nothing much that you can do except tolerate it, even though it is by definition intolerable. Of course, you can go ahead and kill yourself, and I certainly thought enough about doing that, but my will to live and hope for the future was particularly strong, so I somehow tolerated my intensely intolerable state.[7]

My parents were understandably petrified by all of the miserable things that were happening to me, but what else could they do but suffer through it all with me, taking one day at a time? To their supreme credit they were more than willing to do whatever was necessary to help me get better, and I will always appreciate them for that.

---

5. The notion that "crazy" people never get better is a superstition. With the advent of modern ortho-molecular treatment techniques, it is possible to cure a significant proportion of the mentally ill population. Unfortunately, most traditional physicians are either unfamiliar with these techniques or too busy to take the time to seriously implement them.

6. It is precisely for this reason that psychological labeling can be so damaging. For when people find themselves labeled as having a particular disorder, they tend to believe in the label's validity, and this inadvertently causes them to behave as if the label were true. This in turn causes them to become the type of person described by the label, whether they are really that way or not! This in a nutshell is the mysterious phenomenon of self-fulfilling prophecy, and it has more power in our lives than most of us ever realize. As the Bible tells us, we really are what we believe — this is why it is so imperative that we believe positive things about ourselves instead of negative things.

7. On the positive side, being forced to repeatedly tolerate an intolerable state was a good psychological growth exercise for me because it forced me to grow stronger and more understanding with each passing day, just so I could continue to survive.

During all this time I managed to stay in our newly formed band, but my playing ability rapidly deteriorated because of all the prescription drugs I was taking at the hands of my woefully ignorant psychiatrist. I even began to fall asleep during practice sessions because of the tranquilizers, but my good friends and fellow band members did the best they could to put up with the inconvenience.

Then, midway through the winter of the worst year of my life, I found a woman I really loved and who, in return, loved me. Her love and caring gave me a tremendous amount of inner strength and perseverance, so we began going out almost every night. Words simply cannot describe how much she did for me. It was as if she made me whole, and I loved her intensely for that.

Then one evening I had a toxic reaction to all of the tranquilizers I was taking, which caused my shoulder to start jerking up and down uncontrollably. This is a common side effect of the major tranquilizers, but my family doctor decided to put me in the hospital nevertheless.

My shoulder problem cleared up overnight, but they talked me into staying for another three weeks so that I could hopefully get off all the medication I was taking. Reluctantly, I agreed, hoping that someone there would finally be able to find the answer to my ongoing nightmare.

I absolutely hated being there. The daily routines they had us follow were totally nauseous, but I forced myself to follow them anyway, so that I could leave as soon as possible. (Actually, I could have freely left at any time, but to do so would have put me on bad terms with the hospital staff, and I didn't really want to do that.) I found their programs to be extremely poor and far off base in addressing my true problems—as well as the problems of my fellow patients. But as had become characteristic of me, I persevered in the face of outright misery and soon got discharged in good standing, totally withdrawn from all drugs.

Unfortunately, though, my physical problems didn't immediately clear up; they were actually made worse by the drug withdrawal, so I began to take my tranquilizers all over again the very next day. Clearly, the hospital experience wasn't nearly enough to solve my severe health problems.

Soon thereafter, I came to the conclusion that my only hope was to move out to California so that I could undergo Primal Therapy under the direction of Doctor Arthur Janov. I had purchased Doctor Janov's book *The Primal Scream* back in college and ended up liking it so much that I proceeded to memorize almost every page! It made such intuitive sense to me that I came to believe it was my final hope in life.

I talked my girlfriend into moving out with me, and after a good deal of deliberation, she agreed. So did my parents (they really had no choice in the matter, since I appeared to be hopeless otherwise), so by the end of July my girlfriend, her three-year-old daughter, and I were off to California.

On the way out my girlfriend did all sorts of things in my best interest. One thing which stands out most in my mind is when she had a dream one night which told her that I had hidden a tremendous number of pills in the steering column of my car. Armed with this intuitive knowledge she went out in the middle of the night, acted on the information in her dream, and sure enough, there really was a huge cache of pills in the steering column. She then proceeded to get rid of them as soon as possible so she wouldn't be caught—by me or by the police. She hurriedly dumped them into the first place she could find—a duck pond! I had been saving those pills for the "final solution" in case the Primal Therapy didn't work out. But I don't think I ever would have actually taken a fatal dose. I didn't even realize that the pills were gone for another two months!

Once we got out to Los Angeles, finding a suitable place to live was a true ordeal. I could have never done it alone. Fortunately, with the help of some relatives we found a place and got settled. She started going to school and I started my therapy.

The therapy helped me to vent some of my most repressed inner feelings, but the inner sensation of pain in the back of my head persisted, since I continued to take massive quantities of both major and minor tranquilizers. As had become the pattern by then, I proceeded to get worse with each passing day, and I can honestly say that without my compassionate girlfriend and her fun-loving daughter, I never would have been able to make it without a miracle from God. Even as it was, I nearly killed myself on two separate occasions because I was so caught up in my misery.

Then one night, about two years after our arrival in California, I finally reached the end of my rope. I wasn't able to go any further. I agreed with myself that I would pray one final last-ditch prayer to God, and if nothing happened, I would go ahead and kill myself that night one way or another—even if I had to drive my car off a cliff at high speed.

Well, I prayed my prayer at around five o'clock in the morning and basically told God that I couldn't go on another day, and that if He would help me to solve my problem, I would devote the rest of my life to serving Him. As soon as I was done, I opened my eyes and looked around, but nothing happened, so I figured that I would go ahead with my suicidal plans.[8] However, I was much too tired to try to end my life that night, so I decided to put it off until the next day.

Then, incredibly enough, a short two hours after my final, last-ditch prayer I was awakened by a phone call from my cousin Steve, who was a cardiologist in Dallas. He was at the airport in Los Angeles and wanted to come and visit us for a few days.

This caught me totally off guard; after all, I was planning to kill myself later on that day! But now that Steve was in town I couldn't continue thinking such self-destructive thoughts; I had to do my best to be a good host. Consequently, I directly went to pick him up, and from the very first moment I laid eyes on him I knew that something special was going to happen.[9]

As soon as we got home I requested a private meeting with him, so that we could discuss my seemingly hopeless problem. After I explained things to him for a little while, he gave me some very simple advice, but it was advice that was about to change my entire life. He told me how the human brain is by far the most complicated thing we know of, and how I couldn't hope to do anything but screw it up by ingesting so many powerful tranquilizers. In short, he suggested that I give my brain a chance to function solely on its own, because maybe, just maybe, if I did so it would revert back to normal.

This simple bit of advice made immediate intuitive sense to me, because I had been on high doses of prescription tranquilizers for the better part of three years, and I couldn't see how I could feel normal with so many foreign chemicals circulating in my system. So, beginning that very night, I cut the dose of all the drugs I was taking in half. Incredibly enough, the next day I felt much better. At that point I knew that I was on to something big, so I continued cutting back on my daily dose, until soon I wasn't taking anything at all. I also quit smoking and started running at about the same time, largely due to the advice contained in Doctor Marshall Mandell's fabulous book *Dr. Mandell's Five-Day Allergy Relief System.*

It wasn't very easy withdrawing from the various prescription drugs I

---

8. Opting for self-destruction may sound totally irrational, but when a person is faced with an intolerably painful and hopeless disease it suddenly seems like the rational thing to do.

9. It's hard to say whether I would have actually gone ahead and killed myself if Steve hadn't come to visit us. I don't think I would have—I didn't actually want to die, I just wanted the pain to end.

was taking, especially since I was doing it totally on my own, with absolutely no help at all from the medical establishment. I had to put up with some very distressing symptoms for a while, but I soon devised an extremely effective strategy for minimizing these unpleasant withdrawal effects, which I describe in detail later on in this book.[10]

I never imagined that the seemingly innocuous tranquilizers I was taking could cause such distressing withdrawal symptoms. After all, they were prescribed for a legitimate reason by a licensed, well-meaning physician; whoever thought that they could be so darned addicting?

Valium in particular gave me a lot of trouble. I had gotten used to the relatively big doses I was taking every day, so much so that on most days I never even noticed any tranquilizing effect at all from the pills. However, once I started to withdraw I knew that both my brain and body had become exquisitely accustomed to the poison.

The withdrawal process took about a month, but the various psychological symptoms it provoked lasted for over six months! It was terrible, because it was as if my mind was being totally torn apart and slowly reassembled again. To be sure, few things in this world are more frightening that having your own psychological world crumble around you in response to withdrawal, but I tolerated the misery anyway, largely because I had become an expert in tolerating intolerable states of being. (I even continued to make straight A's in the courses I had begun taking, but it took all the strength that I was able to muster.)

Interestingly enough, it was my withdrawal from nicotine which afforded me some of the most dramatic relief that I was ever able to experience during my journey back into health. After a ten-day period of misery following my cessation of smoking, I suddenly experienced a peak of suffering and then an instant and profound cascade of relief. All of a sudden I found myself feeling better than I had felt in years.

Indeed, within a few short weeks of being totally off of all drugs and cigarettes, I began to feel normal again. It was like a miracle: I had been unspeakably miserable for over four years, and now all of a sudden I felt like my old self again.

It was unquestionably the greatest transformation that I had ever been

---

10. I didn't start feeling withdrawal symptoms until several days after cutting back severely on my daily dosage. I had been taking such high doses that it took several days for my tissue level of these drugs to get distressingly low. This is why it felt so good at first to lower my dosage — because I had been taking so much for so long that I was toxic at that high a dosage. Once my tissue level fell significantly below my toxic threshold, however, I started feeling withdrawal symptoms.

through in my entire life. Every single day provided an almost unbelievable amount of psychospiritual progress—and I loved it. I had a lot of catching up to do; after all, I had been out of touch with my real self for over four years, but within a month or two, I was almost totally back to normal.

I now realize that it was all the various poisons that I had taken into my body over a period of years which made me so darned sick. First it was the marijuana, then it was the LSD, the PCP, the hashish, the speed, the cocaine, the Thorazine, the Valium, the antidepressants, and last but not least, all the miserable cigarettes. Indeed, it is no wonder at all that these poisons made me so sick—what's so remarkable is that I somehow managed to get an Associate's Degree in Psychology with highest honors while I was so messed up!

Whoever thought that "recreational" drug use could have such a devastating effect on a person's health? It is important to remember, though, that almost all of my long-term problems were caused by the prescription tranquilizers that I was so naively taking. The marijuana and LSD simply gave me a reason to take those prescription poisons. Indeed, I had been off of all illegal drugs for over three years when I finally decided to get off the tranquilizers.

There's no doubt about it. Seemingly "helpful" tranquilizers such as Valium and Thorazine are, for a lot of people, some of the most evil concoctions ever dreamed up by the mind of man because of their frightening ability to keep a person so far removed from his true self. They are keeping hundreds of thousands of people all over the world imprisoned in a state of zero psychological growth, light years away from their true potential. And what's worse, the vast majority of these people aren't even aware of the fact that most of their problems are caused by the drugs they are taking. This is why tranquilizers can be so evil: because of their ability to wreak such havoc in a person's life, while at the same time causing him to place the blame elsewhere.

However, it wasn't as if everything associated with my withdrawal was negative. On the contrary, I became a much stronger person in all sorts of different ways after the horrible process was over. In fact, I used the temporary crumbling of my cognitive set from the withdrawal to help me get over some of my very worst psychological hangups from childhood. After all, what better way is there to get the mental set that you want than by tearing the whole thing down so that you can build it back up again in the way you find most appropriate?

Significantly enough, the beneficial effects of this personality restructuring have continued down to the present day. I am currently a much calmer person than I ever was before my drug problems began. I am also a good deal more insightful and understanding that I ever would have been had I not gone through my nightmare. It's amazing how much one can grow in response to prodigious suffering.

In fact, I could even go so far as to say that in retrospect I don't regret what happened to me at all, because the tremendous amount of maturity and wisdom that I gained from the struggle more than justified all the suffering I went through. Not that I would ever do it again, or would encourage others to do so, but the end result of all that misery has made my life more enjoyable and productive than it ever would have been otherwise. As the Crucifixion of Christ neatly symbolizes, the best things in life come only through overwhelming suffering. THIS is why I don't regret what happened to me.

However, perhaps the most beneficial aspect of my drug-induced suffering is the psychospiritual awareness and knowledge I was able to acquire as the direct result of my being forced to tolerate such extended bouts of misery. In fact, it was this very knowledge and awareness which has since led me to the primary intellectual passion of my life: the working out of an effective synthesis between Christian theology and depth psychology. I am convinced that this is one of the most important goals in the modern academic world, but without my own "initiation" into the world of suffering, I almost certainly would have never gotten involved with it. Nor would I have been able to understand how the two disciplines actually fit together. There are a good many things in life that one can never fully understand unless one first goes through a period of extended psychospiritual suffering.

Indeed, the years of suffering that I went through have opened up an entirely new realm of philosophical understanding in my mind. I am now able to understand how things in the universe operate and fit together in ways that I would have never understood otherwise. This heightened level of understanding has in turn enabled me to pursue an in-depth writing career and to be happier than I ever would have been otherwise. Consequently, I wouldn't trade the suffering that I experienced for anything else in the entire world.

Unfortunately, though, the story doesn't have a totally happy ending. It turns out that all the various poisons that I consumed over the years greatly damaged my immune system, so that literally overnight I suddenly became hypersensitive to all sorts of common everyday chemicals in the environment. First, it was my girl friend's makeup which began to give me problems, but I soon began to be bothered by cigarette smoke, car exhaust, pesticide spray, and all sorts of other environmental toxins. In fact, there for awhile just about any noxious odor gave me tremendously unpleasant symptoms, ranging all the way from severe migraines to profound fatigue.

Unfortunately for me, this curse of being environmentally sensitive has continued down to the present day, a full decade later. It is an unbelievably miserable problem to have and to be forced to live with. Although dietary supplementation with antioxidant nutrients has helped tremendously, I still am largely defenseless when I am forced to inhale most toxic chemicals. Indeed, I nearly had to be hospitalized while taking a gross anatomy course a couple of years ago because of all the toxic formaldehyde and phenol that the cadavers were preserved with. Consequently, I was forced to wear an extremely uncomfortable and unsightly gas mask to protect myself from the odors during laboratory sessions.[11]

I have been forced to adopt other radical measures to protect myself from all the various toxic exposures in our environment. And while I will hopefully get better as time goes on, I will most likely have to be extremely careful for the rest of my life.

For example, having an intrinsically weak immune system makes me more susceptible to the AIDS virus, assuming that I ever come into contact with it. It has already been shown that in people who have been exposed to the AIDS virus, it is largely the strength of the immune system which determines whether or not a full-blown case of AIDS actually develops. Consequently, I need to be extremely careful to avoid contracting the HIV virus (as we all must be).

A weakened immune system also makes me much more susceptible to cancer formation. It is a well-known fact that the immune system is our first line of defense against cancer; therefore, when the immune system is compromised from excessive drug use, one is much more likely to have a problem with cancer. Unfortunately, it isn't just illicit drug use which damages the immune system; many prescription drugs are also immuno-

---

11. I don't usually react to intrinsically harmless chemicals, like nylon or plastic; I only react to chemicals which are extremely poisonous, such as formaldehyde and chlordane, and which therefore have no business being in our daily environment.

toxic.[12] Hence, many of these prescription drugs could be indirectly contributing to the epidemic of cancer in our society by having a suppressive effect on the immune system.

However, it is the problem of being so darned hypersensitive to the environment which is the biggest curse of having a weakened immune system. It's hard to appreciate just how many toxic chemicals there are in our day-to-day world without being so sensitive to them all. But when the inner quality of your life depends on avoiding a million and one different chemicals, you begin to realize what an impossible chore this avoidance really is.

It is an enormous hassle to have to carefully monitor where you are and what you do just so that an allergy-induced headache doesn't ruin your day. Fortunately, though, I have greatly limited my reactions as of late with the proper diet and a full complement of nutritional supplementation.[13]

I attribute this curse of being so chemically hypersensitive largely to the various licit and illicit drugs I took over approximately five years of time. Indeed, there is mounting experimental evidence indicating that major tranquilizers such as Thorazine and Mellaril can cause much more damage to the immune system than either marijuana or LSD can. I am a living testimony to the reality of this damage.

So as you can see, what began as a daily voyage into ecstasy for me rapidly turned into a constant state of the most profound suffering imaginable. It was only by the Grace of God that I was able to survive. Drugs nearly killed me, and they are killing thousands upon thousands of other drug users every year.

Clearly, something radical needs to be done about this problem as soon as possible, but there is only so much that we as a society can do, since it is the individual user who has ultimate control over the drugs he takes. As anyone who knows a dedicated drug abuser will agree, no addict will ever get better until the addict himself takes the initiative and does whatever it takes to get well. There isn't a doctor or family member in the world who can cure a drug addict: the addict must cure himself. However, before he can do so, two things must happen: (1) he must

---

12. Prescription tranquilizers were responsible for most of the damage to my immune system, not marijuana or LSD. Recent immunotoxic research on these psychiatric drugs has shown several of them to be far more hazardous to the immune system than marijuana or LSD ever could be.

13. The antioxidant mineral selenium in particular has been a tremendous help to me. It has helped me to live with some degree of equanimity in a world that is literally overflowing with toxic chemicals.

sincerely want to change, and (2) he must know how to change. We will be addressing these very issues throughout the remainder of this book.

One final note: It may be legitimately argued that a self-help guide to kicking the drug habit could conceivably be dangerous, since professional medical care is so often indicated in these instances. However, we are not at all suggesting that addicts use the advice in this book at the expense of professional medical care. Without a doubt, if either you or any of your loved ones has a serious drug problem, it is imperative that you get the very best medical help available. After all, drug withdrawal—especially from the hard, physically addicting drugs—is a serious physiological problem which can cause death if it is not properly managed.

On the other hand, most doctors have never kicked the drug habit themselves, so they are woefully unfamiliar with the actual process of withdrawal as it appears from the addict's point of view. In order to be successful, though, a withdrawal program must speak to the individual addict in his own language and on his own terms; otherwise the addict won't be an active part of the treatment process and so will probably relapse when he returns to the street. The bottom line here is that drug rehabilitation isn't an externally administered treatment procedure, like an appendectomy or a liver transplant; it is an internally administered change in attitude and life-style which can only be induced in the addict by an external drug treatment program. To be sure, any true success at rehabilitation, especially in the long term, is due to the patient's *own* knowledge and behavior and not the doctor's.

In other words, the ultimate responsibility for staying off of drugs has to lie with the individual addict himself. After all, the most that any professional detoxification ward can do is to physically wean a person off of drugs and to provide him with the appropriate psychotherapy; after that, it is up to the individual himself to stay clean. But as we have seen time and time again, it is next to impossible for the ex-addict to stay off of drugs indefinitely without some sort of radical change in his thinking and life-style. This is where the material in this book can help: in the educating of the individual addict about the specifics of the drug problem, including the vital areas of withdrawal and rehabilitation.

With this end in mind, we will now get on with our goal by first examining the extent of the drug problem in our society.

Chapter 3

THE SCOPE OF THE PROBLEM

Drug abuse is one of the hottest topics in American politics and social life these days. It consistently rates as the number one area of public concern, ahead of murder, rape, or the threat of nuclear war, and the reason isn't far to seek. Literally millions of precious lives both in this country and abroad are getting ruined every year by drug abuse. We mourned the tragic drug-induced deaths of Len Bias and John Belushi, not just because they were sad in their own right, but because they symbolized the larger problem our society is having with drug abuse.

We are a nation of addicted people. Literally millions upon millions of our nation's citizenry are virtual slaves to some sort of drug habit. And when you include cigarettes, alcohol, caffeine, and sugar in the overall picture, the statistics really become frightening. By these statistics, over 90 percent of our adult population is addicted to some sort of harmful drug.[14]

But that isn't all. An entire illicit industry has sprung up around the extremely lucrative business of drug smuggling. It was recently reported, for example, that the 1986 marijuana crop in Oklahoma was worth over three times the value of its wheat crop, the state's major agricultural product!

Billions upon billions of dollars are being made every year on the international trafficking of marijuana and other drugs. The incentive to smuggle is simple enough to understand: a single individual can easily make several million dollars if he can successfully smuggle a single shipment of cocaine or heroin into this country. It is this huge profit potential, along with the illicit nature of the business in general, which explains why so many underworld figures are attracted to this industry.

Unfortunately, though, it is also this pervasive criminal element which

---

14. The phenomenon of addiction actually extends far beyond the use of addictive chemical substances. True addiction refers to the compulsive use of anything harmful outside of the self which brings relief to a suffering soul. According to this popular definition, even romantic partners can be addicted to one another.

has made drug trafficking one of the most dangerous businesses in the world to be involved in. Hardly a day goes by without our hearing about another drug-involved murder or kidnapping. Why, even the immensely popular show "Miami Vice" was created to portray the profound corruption which permeates virtually the entire drug-smuggling world.

On the international scene, brutal homicides occur almost daily as one drug-smuggling ring or another murders to protect its own best interests. These ruthless individuals torture and kill for revenge and in order to intimidate the police and other opposing factions into leaving them alone, so that they can continue with their unbelievably profitable transactions. Indeed, not long ago one of the heads of the United States Drug Enforcement Agency was brutally tortured and killed while on a government-sponsored mission to Mexico to help quell the tremendous amount of drug trafficking down there. In Columbia, large numbers of judges and scores of other people have been killed by a single group of drug smugglers.

But it isn't as if it is only the criminal element in our society which traffics in mind-altering drugs; the legal pharmaceutical industry is also making billions of dollars peddling prescription psychoactive drugs which are often every bit as dangerous and powerful as illegal drugs are. Indeed, because of consumer demand, there is now a legal pill for just about everything that ails us, ranging from anxiety and depression to hyperactivity and mania. The drug companies of course are taking enormous advantage of our society's current obsession with drugs by creating more mind-altering drugs and by doing more to advertise and distribute them.

From this perspective, then, it isn't surprising at all that we have an illicit drug problem in this country. From childhood onward we are told that there is a pill for just about anything that ails us; illicit drug users simply extend this reasoning to the realm of personal pleasure. Moreover, we Americans have a great deal of trouble delaying gratification. We want to feel good NOW, and so will take just about any pill which promises to make us feel better. And since there are a large number of drugs which can and do generate a tremendous amount of pleasure in the user (at least temporarily), you have the makings of an overwhelming drug problem in this country, involving both prescription and illegal drugs.

NOW is the time for effective action to be taken, before our entire society is crippled by this drug epidemic. If significant headway isn't rapidly made into solving this problem, serious, life-threatening harm will undoubtedly come to a great many people. Why, our very sovereignty as a nation could even be in doubt if too many of our people get chronically impaired by drug abuse. So, with the goal of helping as many people as possible to kick the drug habit, let's now go on to consider exactly why people want to use drugs in the first place.

Chapter 4

WHY DO PEOPLE USE DRUGS?

As we saw in the last chapter, drug abuse has become a literal epidemic both in this country and around the world. Millions upon millions of people are currently abusing psychoactive drugs, as have millions of people down through history. (We are including alcohol in our overall definition of drug abuse, because it is definitely a psychoactive drug that is causing monumental problems in our society.)

With this in mind, why is it that people want to take drugs in the first place? What is it that makes drug use so irresistible to so many people?

Of course, there isn't any one reason why people use drugs; there are several reasons which act together, with certain reasons being more applicable than others for each abusing individual. Thus, the best way to understand the motivation of the drug abuser is to examine each contributing factor separately.

To begin with, there is the factor of man's intrinsic slothfulness to consider. Human beings characteristically desire the easiest way out of most problems; it is a fundamental tendency which seems to be built into our very nature.[15] For most people, though, life itself is the greatest problem of all. Consequently, most individuals are constantly on the lookout for some type of shortcut "solution" to the problem of life. Unfortunately, for millions of people the use of drugs is the easiest way around the problem of life.

The reason for this has to do with tremendous importance of feeling good in human life. Most people tend to use the criterion of how well they are feeling deep inside to gauge how well they are actually solving the problem of life. If they feel good, they figure that they are being

---

15. The molecules of which we are made also are "lazy" in the sense that they too desire the lowest energy state in which to exist. Perhaps this is one reason why we humans naturally tend to be lazy—because the physical building blocks of which we are made are also lazy.

pretty successful at solving the problem of life, but if they feel bad, they figure that they aren't being very successful at it. The subsequent tie-in with drug abuse is twofold: (1) people naturally tend to feel bad from time to time; and (2) drugs are almost miraculous in their capacity to make a person who is feeling bad temporarily feel better. From these two considerations alone it logically follows that many people will come to see drug abuse as a legitimate way of solving the problem of life, since it satisfies their fundamental prerequisite for successful living: feeling good deep inside.

What these people need to realize is that there are two ways to feel good in life: the legitimate way, through honest effort and hard work, and the illegitimate way, through the simple popping of a pill or the downing of some booze. Feeling good may thus be an indication that one is being successful at solving the problem of life, but only if it comes the legitimate way, through honest effort and hard work; if it comes the illegitimate way, through drug or alcohol abuse, severe problems will inevitably result.

Thus, the drug-abusing personality type is by definition more likely to seek the illegitimate, shortcut road to personal happiness through the use of drugs than the legitimate road which entails honest effort and hard work. Unfortunately for the abuser, though, such skimping is not without consequence. Indeed, when one repeatedly takes advantage of one's free will and the bio-circuitry of the brain by achieving a false ecstasy with drugs, true happiness will remain forever elusive; in its place will come poor physical and mental health, an empty pocketbook, and a generally messed up life.

4.1 Why Teenagers Use Drugs

Teenagers make up a significant percentage of drug users. Although they are driven to use drugs and alcohol by many of the same reasons which motivate adults, teens are also motivated by several additional factors which are characteristic of adolescence.

The chief adolescent characteristic which most predisposes teens to drug and alcohol abuse is undoubtedly their native rebelliousness. All teenagers go through a stage of rebelliousness against authority; it is a normal stage of human development. Teens get into trouble, though, when they express their rebelliousness through the use of drugs and alcohol.[16]

A better way for teens to express their rebelliousness is by flaunting authority through more legitimate means, such as by listening to bizarre music, coloring their hair green, or by taking up a strange new hobby that their parents disapprove of. Developing one's psychological independence from one's parents may be important, but it isn't so important that it justifies risking one's health and future over it with drugs.

4.1.1 The Essence of Spite

Spite is an extremely powerful motivating force in human life, especially for the teenager. It naturally grows out of the teenager's inner tendency to rebel and can quickly become malignant if it is routinely provoked by angry parents.

The essence of spite is to be found in the delicate nature of the teenager's developing identity structure. It comes into play when the teen's extremely fragile sense of personal identity is routinely challenged by ruthless parental criticism. Thus, when parents repeatedly negate a teenager's person, value, and integrity by violently opposing something he is doing, it is only natural for the teen to want to spite his parents by doing exactly what they don't want him to do. If the object of parental opposition is drug abuse, for instance, the youth will oftentimes want to use drugs more than ever, just to spite the parents.

On a deeper level, the essence of spite has to do with the critical process of identity differentiation between parents and children. When parents overly criticize their children, they inadvertently criticize the psychospiritual identity that their children have attained for themselves; this is subsequently perceived by the children as an overt rejection of who they really are deep inside. This rejection in turn threatens them with the loss of their precious inner identity—which is already extremely fragile and tenuous to begin with—because the happiness of their parents seems to depend on the abandonment of their criticized behavior, and hence of the identity which originally chose to engage in it. The implicit assumption on the part of the teenager seems to be that since he is the one who actually chose to engage in the criticized behavior, it can't

---

16. Every year we seem to read about at least one teenager who inadvertently dies after trying to "chug" an entire fifth of whiskey or vodka in a drinking race. Needless to say, this is a profoundly dangerous thing for anyone to attempt, because death is so often the tragic result. Ethyl alcohol is a powerful central nervous system depressant, so it can easily kill a person when too much of it is consumed in a short period of time.

be "wrong" without his inner identity also being "wrong," i.e. he figures that since his identity is so tied into whatever he is doing wrong that it is automatically rejected along with his behavior, he can't give up the behavior without simultaneously giving up who he really is deep inside.

A critical choice thus unconsciously presents itself to the severely criticized child sooner or later: whether to abandon his identity by doing what his parents want him to do, or to preserve his identity by doing exactly what they don't want him to do. If his self-confidence is strong enough, he will usually choose to maintain his identity by being spiteful. If it isn't strong enough, he will usually succumb to his parents' wishes and sacrifice his true inner self in the process.[17]

In other words, in order to keep from losing the identity that he has worked so hard for, the spiteful child will choose to bolster it by doing the exact opposite of whatever his parents tell him to do. Again, the implicit assumption seems to be that if his identity is so tied into whatever he is doing wrong that it is automatically rejected along with his behavior, he can then enhance his identity by doing wrong even more. To give in would thus mean to sacrifice his inner initiative and self-will, and to lose part of his precious identity in the process, and this is understandably a fate worse than death for most normal adolescents. This is how tremendously important their identity is to them—they would much rather risk their lives in order to retain their identity than risk their identity in order to retain their lives.

Spite is actually a good sign in growing children, because it means that they haven't abandoned their struggle to develop a unique and totally independent identity for themselves. The time to worry is when a child routinely sacrifices his true inner self in order to make his parents happy, because this invariably leads to severe psychological problems later on in life.

The key to preventing spiteful behavior in children is to avoid threatening their delicate identity structure with overly negative criticism. This involves the single most important skill in all of childraising: being able to reject a child's behavior without simultaneously rejecting his inner person. This is admittedly a difficult skill to learn, but it is nonetheless critical that it be learned anyway, because the child's present

---

17. This type of self-sacrificial behavior inevitably leads to hostility, resentment, and other neurotic symptoms later in life. A person simply cannot smother his true inner self without suffering severe and lasting consequences because of it.

behavior and future psychological well-being depends largely on how well it is implemented by his parents.

There are a variety of effective techniques for helping a child to feel loved and accepted when his behavior is simultaneously being rejected. They all involve the notion of unconditional positive regard, which is basically the technique of openly loving a child no matter what he does. It doesn't mean liking or accepting whatever the child does, though; it only means not making your love dependent on what the child does; it means continuing to openly love a child while he is still simultaneously being criticized. When this is done, the child's fragile identity is automatically separated from your criticism of his behavior. This in turn leads to three beneficial consequences: (1) it makes the child much more likely to listen to what you have to say; (2) it leads to an eventual elimination of spiteful behavior; and (3) it makes future neurotic development much less likely, because it reduces the need of the child to sacrifice his inner self in order to make his parents happy.

As far as the actual process of safely criticizing a child is concerned, there are several specific techniques one can use to advantage. They include being positive with the child as much as possible, criticizing in a positive way, and not being overly rejecting and moralistic during family squabbles. However, perhaps the most effective way of safely criticizing a child is by establishing a loving and mutually respectful relationship with him when he is not being criticized. This can be achieved by habitually respecting the child's needs and feelings and by doing whatever else you can to let him know that he is loved, no matter what he does. Routinely addressing him with a loving nickname always seems to help, especially when he is being actively criticized. In this way a general foundation of love and acceptance can be laid with the child, so that whenever behavioral criticisms do arise, they will occur over against a positive emotional backdrop; this in turn will help to keep the child's fragile identity structure intact while his behavior is getting criticized.

4.1.2 The Larger Implications of the Teenager's Incessant Struggle for Identity

Interestingly enough, teenagers are actually on the right track when they take their identity formation so seriously, because the whole purpose of life seems to be centered around the process of developing a mature and independent psychospiritual identity for oneself. This is apparently why we must go through a gradual process of self-guided psychospiritual development in life: because it is only by gaining our knowledge and development on our own through our own free-willed behavior in the world that we can gain an independent identity for ourselves. This is undoubtedly why we must start out life as naive infants: because any thorough process of identity formation must start out from the very beginning of the human developmental process, so that the individual can gain all of his knowledge and development on his own.[18]

The existence of human evil also seems to be related to the process of psychospiritual identity formation in man. God apparently allows human evil to exist because it seems to be an inescapable part of the human "definition," at least during man's initial developmental stages. That is to say, human evil seems to be largely caused by the fact that man is still only partially developed at the present time,[19] but this partial assembly is absolutely necessary, at least temporarily, if man is to be capable of attaining an independent identity for himself. Again, this is because an independent psychospiritual identity can only be attained when man gradually gains his own knowledge and development for himself. Thus, partial character development, along with the evil it naturally produces, is an essential prerequisite for man to be fully human, but only temporarily; once man finally reaches his cosmic goal and becomes fully developed, the evil that was originally caused by his partial assembly will disappear by definition.

In other words, God allows human evil to temporarily exist on this planet because it is a necessary means to the much greater end of independent identity formation in man. This is why God could not instantaneously create man by Divine Fiat: because to do so would automatically violate the most important part of the human definition— that of humans gaining their own knowledge and development on their own and of gaining an independent identity in the process.[20] From this

---

18. There are a variety of complex reasons for this dependence of human identity formation on a self-guided process of development, but they are far beyond the scope of this book. I plan to discuss these reasons in detail in a later work.

19. All partially assembled objects malfunction by their very nature when they are operated in a partially assembled state. Man is no different. In the same way that a partially assembled automobile would naturally wreck if it were driven on a busy highway, partially assembled man naturally wrecks in life by committing behavioral evil, because all the essential "working parts" for preventing evil are not yet present in his soul.

20. Saying that God was "unable" to create man without simultaneously creating the propensity for evil doesn't limit God's Power at all. As I show elsewhere, it is logically impossible for man to exist without the temporary propensity for evil also existing, and God's Power cannot be limited by logical impossibilities.

point of view, it is apparent that the only way God could abolish human evil on this planet is by instantly giving man all the knowledge and development he would ever need in order to be able to behave correctly, but this is unacceptable because it would automatically transform man into a preprogrammed robot, which in turn would automatically destroy any hope for a self-attained (and therefore for a uniquely human) identity structure.

4.1.3 Teens and Peer Pressure

Another often-cited reason why teens begin using drugs is peer pressure. It is easy to downplay the awesome power of peer pressure, but the fact remains that it is perhaps the most powerful factor of all in determining who uses drugs and who doesn't. If you're in junior high or high school and all of your friends are using drugs, it is next to impossible to resist using them yourself. After all, the desire to belong and be popular is one of the strongest motivating factors in a teenager's life. Thus, if a teenager's acceptance into a highly valued social clique is dependent on his using drugs, he is definitely at risk, especially if he is being repeatedly goaded by his friends into conformity. Teens only possess a certain amount of inner resolve and willpower; when that inner reserve gets overtaxed, drug abuse is a likely consequence.

It is extremely difficult for parents to protect their children against the corrupting power of peer pressure. They can try to make sure that their children will only be exposed to the "nicest," non-drug-using children, but this is next to impossible, since drug abuse happens in even the best of families and schools. Also, it is virtually impossible to control who our children come into contact with outside the home.

It is possible, however, to bolster our children's inner resistance to the corrupting effects of peer pressure. This can be done in several ways:

1. By educating them in detail about the many dangers which are inherent in drug use. Here, it is important not to exaggerate, because if they find your information to be incorrect, they may not believe any of it. If it can be arranged, a trip to a local detoxification ward can discourage future drug use if it is done properly, without incrimination.

2. By strengthening their self-image in such a way that they don't feel the need to conform to anyone else's wishes in order to feel worthwhile. Help them to feel good about themselves even though you may disagree with their thinking or behavior.

3. By allowing them to feel free to discuss their problems with you at any time without the fear of undue hostility or punishment.

4.1.4 Boredom and Drug Abuse

Another major reason why people abuse drugs involves one of mankind's most aggravating problems: boredom. People have been bored at one time or another since the dawn of human history, but now, with the advent of so many time and labor-saving devices, we in modern-day America have more free time on our hands than ever before. And since very few of us are creative enough to use this free time in a persistently constructive fashion, we are extremely prone to the hazardous effects of boredom.

Boredom can be exceedingly dangerous for the following simple reason: the human mind is designed to operate at a relatively high level of conscious functioning. Thus, when boredom reduces this level of functioning to a bare minimum, the mind gets restless and begins looking for stimulation outside of itself. And since illicit stimulation (through drug and alcohol abuse) is so much easier to obtain than legitimate stimulation (through mountain climbing or marathon running), boredom provides a fertile breeding ground for all types of drug and alcohol abuse.

Teenagers are especially prone to the hazardous effects of boredom for two major reasons: First, because most teens are still being supported by their parents, they typically have a great deal of free time on their hands, and this is usually more than enough for them to get bored on a daily basis. Secondly, the teenage mind by its very nature looks for a high level of excitement and stimulation in life. Consequently, when a severe case of boredom sets in, the teenager becomes doubly motivated to look for excitement in drug abuse.

Fortunately, the problem of teenager boredom can be dealt with in a variety of constructive ways. For one thing, our high schools can get a lot more demanding, so that students will be forced to put out a much greater effort at home in order to pass or do well. This alone will greatly reduce the amount of boredom in their lives. Another way to deal with the problem of teenage boredom involves employment: parents can require their teens to have a part-time job while they are in school. Having a part-time job not only gives kids a sense of responsibility and some extra cash, it also keeps them out of trouble by greatly reducing the amount of boredom in their lives.

4.1.5 Stress and Drug Abuse

Another major component to the teenager's (as well as the adult's) desire to use drugs involves stress reduction. We are all under a tremendous amount of stress here in the latter part of the twentieth century. We are under physical stress, chemical stress, radiation stress, and financial stress, not to mention the mental and emotional stress which emanates from loneliness, divorce, arguments, and various inner conflicts.

In order to maintain proper psychobiological equilibrium, we need to dissipate the psychophysiological effects of stress at regular intervals. The healthy way to do this is through such activities as running, meditation, yoga, and the psychological purging of our repressed pains and fears. The unhealthy way is through the use of such "anti-stress" drugs as Valium, Librium, and the whole gamut of illegal drugs.

It is easy to understand why so many people opt to reduce the stress in their lives through drug abuse than through aerobic exercise or meditation. Exercise and meditation require considerable effort, while popping a pill requires almost no effort at all. Remember, people are basically lazy, so they will choose the easy way out of a problem nine times out of ten. However, the easy way out almost never provides genuine satisfaction; true success at almost anything requires a legitimate amount of effort, and this applies to stress reduction as much as it does to anything else.

Parents should try to minimize the amount of stress in their children's lives as much as possible if they want to do their best to keep their children drug-free. But since record numbers of children are having to tolerate divorce, alcoholic parents, and strife within the family, record numbers of children are beginning to use drugs and alcohol.

We must never forget that children are not nearly as well equipped as adults are to deal with severe emotional stress in their lives. They are young, naive, and often extremely vulnerable; hence, when a major trauma occurs in their lives, they are likely to become severely affected by it. Consequently, parents need to be very sensitive to their children's emotional needs, so they can help them out whenever their children are feeling particularly bad. Otherwise, if they are left alone to deal with their feelings in whatever way they see fit, they are likely to turn to drugs and/or alcohol for relief.

If extreme stress is unavoidable in our children's lives, we adults need to go out of our way to provide them with acceptable methods of coping with the pain and suffering. This could mean membership to a health club, daily swimming at the local "Y," or regular breaks or vacations away from the source of the stress.

However, perhaps the most effective way parents can reduce the emotional stress in their children's lives is simply by listening to them with a sympathetic and uncritical ear. We must never underestimate the power of a good rap session in eliminating emotional stress from our lives. Indeed, teenagers are just like adults, in that they typically feel much better after they bounce their problems off a sympathetic listener. Moreover, if the teen sees that his parents are genuinely interested in him and are supportive of his problems, this very fact will dissipate a good deal of the stress; he will perceive that at the very least his own parents are on his side.

There's no doubt about it: parents need to communicate effectively with their children if they want them to grow up in a healthy and mature fashion. A great many parents hardly even know their children apart from a few irrelevant trivialities, so parents, get to know your children. Discuss their problems regularly with them and you will be amazed how much better they will be because of it.

Of course, the most important aspect to establishing good rapport with one's children is the ability to give unconditional love to them no matter what they do. If we do, our children will feel MUCH less pressured and MUCH less stressed, since they will realize that they don't have to struggle to get their parents' love. In turn, they will respond by performing better in all aspects of their lives, since all children want to be loved for who they really are and not for what they can do to make their parents happy.[21]

4.1.6 More Reasons for Teenage Drug Abuse

Another reason for teenage drug use involves the modeling of their behavior after the behavior of their parents and the rest of our adult society. Teenagers tend to model their behavior after the behavior of our adult society, because one of their most difficult developmental tasks is to be able to successfully enter the adult world. Unfortunately, we live in a drug-obsessed culture, pure and simple, so it is only natural for kids to want to imitate normal adult behavior by smoking, drinking, and taking pills.

Parents can minimize this unhealthy modeling effect by not smoking, drinking, or taking drugs themselves. In this way children grow up learning that drugs are not the solution to life's problems; consequently, they are less likely to resort to drugs themselves when things get difficult in their own lives. Certainly, it is woefully inadequate to tell our chil-

---

21. As we have already seen, it is often extremely difficult to be able to reject a child's behavior while simultaneously loving and accepting HIM. Unless it is done properly, though, most children interpret a rejection of their behavior as a rejection of THEM, and this in turn can lead to all sorts of psychological problems later on in life.

dren to stay off of drugs when we have a cigarette in one hand and a martini in the other! Teenagers are extremely sensitive to any hypocrisy at all on the part of their parents and the rest of society.

However, perhaps the most powerful motivating factor behind drug use is the reinforcing effect of the drugs themselves. Most illicit psychoactive drugs make the user feel incredibly good (at least for a time) and it is this good feeling which is so reinforcing. Since it feels so good, the user tends to want to repeat the experience indefinitely.

This phenomenon of drug-reinforced behavior happening more frequently can be demonstrated with rats. When rats are given the choice between punching a lever for food and punching a lever for cocaine, they will repeatedly choose the cocaine until they literally starve themselves to death. The reason of course is that the cocaine is much more reinforcing to the rat than food is, so it chooses cocaine.

A good alternative to the tremendous reinforcing power of drug abuse is to find effective substitutes for the drug-induced pleasure in one's life. Vigorous aerobic exercise is a great alternative. Exercising on a regular basis causes endogenous painkilling chemicals called endorphins to be released in the body, and it is this release which causes the athlete to feel so good, both while he is exercising and afterwards. Indeed, it is precisely this endorphin release which is the primary cause of the famed "runner's high."

I used to be skeptical myself about runner's high, that is, until I actually started running. When I had my very first runner's high soon thereafter, I knew that I was going to be a runner for the rest of my life. Running made me feel that good. In fact, it made me feel so much better that I naturally wondered how I had ever tolerated feeling so bad and so sluggish for so long! To be sure, runner's high (or swimmer's high, or whatever the case may be) is just as reinforcing as drug abuse is, and even more so, since it is an acceptable way to feel good; hence, once you get it, you are going to want to get it again and again. This is a major reason why serious athletes are so addicted to their daily exercise—because it makes them feel so much better.

This brings us to one of the most powerful strategies for avoiding drug addiction: finding a positive addiction to take its place. We all know of positive addictions: running, swimming, cycling, walking, traveling, and the like. Once we find the appropriate positive addiction for us the lure from drugs will be next to nonexistent, because our inner need for a source of gratification will be satisfied.

4.1.7 The Relationship Between Addictive Personalities and Drug Abuse

In any serious attempt to understand why people use drugs, it is important to realize that many of us have an inner predisposition to addiction. In psychiatry, this is termed an "addictive personality." The addictive personality may gravitate towards alcohol, other psychoactive drugs, gambling, or addictive relationships to ease his pain, but whatever he chooses, he becomes addicted to it.

There seem to be two different motivating factors behind the classic addictive personality. On the one hand, his personality structure may be so weak that he needs a constant supply of his drug just in order to keep from falling apart. This qualifies such an individual as a pathologically dependent personality, with drug use being the object of his dependence.

These people tend to look for their fulfillment in areas outside their own selves. Such a dependency object may or may not initially be drugs or alcohol; it could just be a job or a spouse. But once these dependency objects are lost, the addictive personality feels driven to use some other type of dependency object to substitute for them. Drugs and alcohol remain two of the most popular ways of performing this substitution.

Of course, there are many relatively normal people who only turn to drug abuse when a major part of their life—such as a marriage or lifelong art project—fails in some way. This type of failure can lead to a profound depression which in turn can destroy a person's initiative and motivation for success, at least for a time. Such individuals still want to succeed; they just don't want to invest any more effort into attaining their goal, because they usually don't have any more effort to invest.

Many of these profoundly demoralized people turn to drug and alcohol abuse as a way of feeling better in the face of their misery. Once their failure is deemed absolute, they consolidate their various strivings and desires into a chemical habit which at least makes them temporarily feel like they are being successful.[22] Thus, instead of having to worry about producing the perfect painting or making their spouse happy, all they have to worry about is taking the right drug at the right time and in the right manner. This greatly simplifies their lives but only temporarily and only in a defeatist sort of way.

It isn't entirely clear whether a chemical addiction which results in this manner is due the addictive nature of the individual's personality,

---

22. Substance abuse makes people feel successful to the extent that it gives them the sense of euphoria which normally accompanies success in life.

to his depression, or to some combination of both. There is certainly the potential for depression in most addictive personalities; after all, the addicted person is utterly dependent on his chosen object and so is constantly intimidated by the threat of its potential loss. This fear alone is capable of causing a severe depression in addicted people. The lack of personal independence in such individuals is also capable of inducing a severe depression, because it is depressing to have to be enslaved to some type of object outside of oneself. Worst of all, though, is the depression which results when addicted individuals actually lose the object of their dependency. It is often so bad that only a powerful chemical substance can help to alleviate their pain and suffering.

On the other hand, extreme failure-induced depression can lead to chronic substance abuse in people who are not normally addictive. Clearly, depression and drug abuse often go hand in hand.

The classic addictive personality can also be motivated by a passionate desire for peak experiences. This is seen most often in those with "extremist" personalities, as opposed to those whose lives are controlled by cautiousness and moderation. Now since the world of substance abuse offers literally one peak experience after another, it is easy to see why such an individual could easily get addicted to drugs or alcohol.

If you suspect that you have an addictive personality, you should seek out professional treatment as soon as possible before you get yourself into any more trouble. Treatment revolves around determining the originating factor behind one's proclivity to addiction. In the case of dependent addictive personalities, the treatment involves lessening their need for dependence by strengthening their overall personality structure. In the case of extremist addictive personalities, the treatment involves finding a constructive substitute which is able to offer similar types of peak experiences. In both cases, finding a useful positive addiction can be a tremendous help, if not an outright cure.

4.2 Drug Use as a Temporary Developmental Stage

There are various stages of development which we routinely grow through on our way to mature adulthood. Many of these stages have extremely unpleasant components to them. This is why we tend to think that many of the people we know who are experiencing a personal crisis are only going through some type of temporary "phase" in their lives. And more often than not, such crises really are due at least in part to these developmental phases. Not surprisingly, drug use can also be seen as a temporary developmental phenomenon in many people.

Many people seem to go through a "normal" phase of drug use on their way to mature adulthood. While this pattern is seen most often in marijuana smokers and beer drinkers, it is also seen in multiple drug users as well. For instance, a great many people smoke pot and/or take drugs for a period of time—usually in high school and college—and then quit or taper down a great deal once they get a little older.

The reason most often cited for this type of decline in drug use over time has to do with the actual quality of the highs that are experienced: Many people report that their highs progressively got much more unpleasant as they got older, with the direct consequence that they either severely curtailed their drug use or quit entirely.

Such individuals appear to have actually outgrown the desire to use drugs. When this is the case, the drug use that formerly existed can be viewed as a temporary developmental phase that the individual was going through.

Oftentimes, though, this type of phase-induced drug use results in a physical addiction. If and when this occurs and the addiction is serious, it is important to realize that only the inner developmental need to use drugs will have dissipated when the phase is outgrown; the individual will still need to continue using drugs to satisfy his physical addiction. In these cases only a strong desire to kick the drug habit will enable the individual to break free of his addiction once and for all.

Some people never seem to outgrow the use of drugs. Being a lifelong user of a particular drug, however, doesn't necessarily make a person mentally unbalanced. After all, there are literally millions of relatively normal people who smoke and drink into old age, and their ongoing drug use isn't indicative of anything worse than desiring to have a good time on a regular basis. On the other hand, in many other individuals a lifelong drug habit is indicative of some type of severe character disorder. The fundamental criterion for determining the psychological healthiness of such an individual is directly related to how much he lets his drug habit dominate his life: the more dominance, the unhealthier it is for him.

As always, though, quitting is the important thing. Ironically, allowing one's life to be dominated by drug use can turn out to be a good thing in the long run, since it can lead to an intensely bad experience which in turn can eventually lead to a healthy personality transformation and a complete cessation of drug use.

4.3 Normal vs. Abnormal Drug Use

As we would naturally expect, different people use drugs for different reasons. Some of these reasons are compatible with psychological normality, while others are indicative of psychological abnormality. In the more "abnormal" phases of drug use, the user derives virtually his entire identity from his drug habit. Of course, the extent of this identity domination depends on the strength of the personality structure to begin with: the weaker the user's personality structure originally was, the more dominated he will typically be by his drug habit. Conversely, the stronger the user's personality structure originally was, the less dominated he will typically be by his drug habit. Hence, only those individuals with pathologically weak personality structures will allow their entire identities to be dependent on their drug habit.

The more abnormal drug user will tend to use drugs far more often during the day, while the more psychologically healthy user will only get high every other day or even just on weekends. Again, this is a direct reflection on the inner strength and healthiness of the personality structure: the weaker the personality structure is, the more often one is likely to use drugs.

Many persons with underlying psychological problems use depressant drugs on a daily basis to help them deal with a part of themselves they don't want to face. Such individuals are generally having a great deal of trouble with their repressions, so they feel driven to resort to drug abuse to help them maintain their overall repressive status. These are the people who are most dependent on their drug of choice, because their psychological stability absolutely depends on it. This is why such individuals dread the unavailability of their chosen poison—not because they are particularly afraid of withdrawal per se, but because they are afraid of coming face-to-face with an unwanted part of themselves which they've never known and which therefore absolutely terrifies them.

This unwanted part of the personality is known in Jungian psychology as the shadow. It is comprised of all those thoughts and feelings which have been banished to the unconscious because of their apparent threat to the ego. However, the shadow isn't really bad; it only appears to be bad because of all the unpleasant feelings which are associated with it. These unpleasant feelings come into play when an essential part of the personality is rejected by the ego.[23] Such a rejection sets up a constant state of tension between the shadow, which wants to rise to the surface so it can be reintegrated into the personality structure, and the ego, which wants to keep it banished to the unconscious forever. Thus, the shadow is really good, because it is an essential part of the personality; it only appears to be bad as long as it is rejected. Consequently, before true mental health can be achieved, the shadow must be consciously faced and integrated into the overall personality structure.

The average neurotic individual, though, doesn't recognize his shadow as being good. He only sees it as a horrible Enemy that is to be avoided at all cost, so he does whatever he can to keep it buried in his unconscious. However, since it is an essential part of his personality, the shadow is always struggling for release so it can rejoin the personality structure and make it whole again. Psychological problems result when bits and pieces of the shadow begin to break through the repressive process and seep into conscious awareness.

When this occurs, the individual becomes a red-hot candidate for drug or alcohol abuse, since most depressant drugs act to bolster the repressive process (at least temporarily). If substance abuse is succumbed to in such a circumstance, it is done virtually guilt-free, because as far as the abuser is concerned, the drugs are being taken for a legitimate reason: that of maintaining overall psychological stability.[24] This is why neurotic drug users are the most addicted people of all — because their daily psychological stability appears to absolutely depend on it.

It is important to realize, though, that this apparent stability is just an illusion. The only thing which remains stable in such a circumstance is the neurotic process itself. In contrast, true mental health can only be achieved when repressive drugs are abandoned and the shadow is faced on its own terms in all its horrible intensity, for it is only in this way that the personality can be made whole once and for all. In this sense the neurotic drug user paradoxically must first lose control before he can gain control; he must lose control of his neurotic struggle so that his shadow can subsequently be released and reintegrated into the conscious

---

23. This transformation in the character of rejected psychic material is a manifestation of a psychological law which says that if any part of the original personality is rejected by the ego, the rejected part tends to turn demonic until it is re-accepted into consciousness.

24. Indeed, if he goes to see a psychiatrist he will usually receive a prescription for a tranquilizer which does the same thing that most illicit drugs do — keep the shadow repressed. Psychiatric drugs "tranquilize" by aiding the overall repressive process.

whole. When this occurs, he will finally gain control of a much healthier personality.

4.3.1 Why Different People Respond to the Same Drugs in Different Ways

Although there are many individuals who are capable of taking psychoactive drugs without suffering much problem, there are many others who have terrible reactions to the very same drugs. Similarly, while there are some individuals who don't seem to be harmed by the regular use of drugs, there are others who are harmed a great deal by just occasional use. In this section we will attempt to explain why drug reactions vary so tremendously from person to person.

To begin with, some people seem to be hypersensitive or allergic to a given drug. Thus, whenever they attempt to use it, they suffer an allergic-type reaction which is far out of proportion to the drug's usual effects. Although this type of allergic response may in fact be due to some type of oversensitive psychological process in the mind, it is usually the result of an idiosyncratic biochemical hypersensitivity in the brain.

A more prevalent reason for the vast differences seen in drug response has to do with a person's inner motivation for taking drugs. It appears as though the amount of harm a given drug has on an individual is largely dependent on the underlying reason why the drug is being taken, i.e. it isn't always the frequency of use or the chemical nature of a given drug which is most harmful to an individual; it is the specific inner purpose the drug is being used for which is capable of inflicting the most harm. As the old saying goes, guns don't kill people—people do. Likewise, drugs in and of themselves don't always hurt people—people do, with the maladaptive things they inadvertently do to themselves with drugs.

For instance, if a drug is being used only occasionally, not for any deep psychological purpose, but only for a good time, the harm it causes will probably be relatively small and usually only in direct proportion to the drug's frequency of use and specific chemical nature.[25] On the other hand, if a drug is routinely used as a chemical tool for dealing with an individual's inner psychopathology, the harm it causes is likely to be far worse, not just because it is being used more, but because it is being used to manipulate a ferocious inner illness. Indeed, it is the illness itself, and not the drug, which causes the majority of problems in these cases; the drug only serves to unleash the formidable power which is tied up in the

---

25. Of course, this isn't to say that the recreational use of drugs is harmless; it is just relatively harmless when compared to the more serious, psychotherapeutic use of drugs.

illness. This is why so many people eventually crack up when they use drugs for this type of inner "therapeutic" purpose: because each time a mind-altering drug is used to "treat" an inner psychological problem, the problem tends to get worse and worse.

However, it isn't as if the only people who have aversive reactions to drugs are those who use them for inner psychotherapeutic reasons. There are many other people who don't knowingly use drugs at all for this purpose but who still have bad reactions to the very same drugs nonetheless. Indeed, there are large numbers of people who have experienced a dramatic change in their own response to a particular drug over time.

This difference in subjective drug response in different people, and in the same person over time, is a curious phenomenon which has yet to be fully explained in the psychiatric literature. However, our psychoanalytic paradigm has something to contribute on this issue. It appears as though the main reason for this difference in drug response has something to do with an individual's current repressive status, which can be expressed as a particular location on the Repression-Unrepression Continuum (see Figure 1). The closer an individual is to the repressed end of the continuum, the less jostled his internal repressive apparatus is likely to be; hence, a given depressant drug will probably be successful in helping him to solidify his overall repressive status, and this in turn will probably make him feel better, at least for a time.

Figure 1

The Repression – Unrepression Continuum and its Relation to Specific Drug Effects

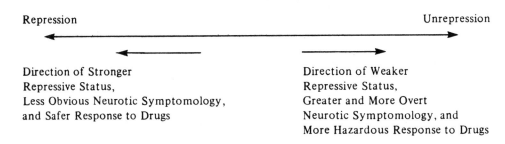

On the other hand, the closer an individual is to the unrepressed end of the continuum, the more jostled his internal repressive apparatus is likely to be; hence, a given depressant drug will probably have more trouble trying to solidify his overall repressive status, and this in turn will probably make him feel a good deal worse, at least for a time. Indeed, if his inner "repressive lid" has been sufficiently tampered with (say with long-term marijuana or LSD use), attempting to strengthen the repressive process with drugs could cause the entire repressive apparatus to gyrate wildly out of control. By the same token, when an individual's repressive ability has been compromised in some way, he is generally more sensitive to all types of drugs, including stimulants and especially hallucinogens. This is because his unconscious emotional pain has been partially liberated and so therefore has much greater access to conscious awareness. Thus, when a given stimulant or hallucinogen is consumed by an individual who is having trouble with his repressions, his unconscious emotional pain is directly affected by the drug, because it has been partially released from its unconscious "prison." If the drug is a central nervous system depressant, it will tend to suppress the liberated pain for a time. When the drug effect wears off, however, the pain suppression will usually give way to an unpleasant "rebound" effect, which occurs when the partially repressed pain takes an even greater-than-normal leap into conscious awareness. It is this rebound effect which appears to cause the majority of bad reactions in people who react aversively to depressant drugs.

On the other hand, LSD, marijuana, and other hallucinogens affect this partially liberated pain much more directly. Because these drugs biochemically interfere with the repressive process, they directly act to increase the amount of unconscious pain which reaches conscious awareness. This is why individuals who are having trouble with their repressions generally have bad reactions to the various hallucinogenic drugs. It also appears to be why some people initially react positively to LSD or marijuana and then gradually find that their reactions become more and more negative over time: because at first their unconscious pain is much more securely repressed and so is not directly affected by their initial drug use. Continued use, however, leads to a biochemically induced weakening of their inner repressive process, which in turn partially liberates a certain amount of unconscious pain. It is this pain which makes later drug use so unpleasant—because of the pain's greater proximity to consciousness, it is much more directly stimulated by these drugs than it was before. This in turn causes the pain (and the suffering it generates) to leap higher and higher into conscious awareness.

Now we are in a position to understand why the serious psychotherapeutic use of a given drug is usually so much more hazardous than flippant, casual use: because the serious user is much more likely to reside on the unrepressed end of the Repression-Unrepression Continuum and is therefore more likely to have his pain be directly exposed to the drug's biochemical effects. The casual user, on the other hand, is more likely to reside on the repressed end of the Repression-Unrepression Continuum, and this makes it more likely that his unconscious pain will be more effectively shielded from a given drug's biochemical effects. Hence, it is the proximity of a person's repressed pain to consciousness which seems to determine both the degree of harm and the type of reaction a person experiences on a given drug: the closer the pain is to consciousness, the worse the reaction and the greater the harm that is usually incurred.

Paradoxically, though, these "bad" drug reactions can be seen as being "good" in the long run for the following two reasons: (1) bad reactions generally motivate people to quit taking drugs once and for all; and (2) bad reactions signify a partial liberation of unconscious pain, which itself is a necessary first step towards a final resolution of the pain.

The upshot of this discussion is simply this: if a person is having trouble managing his inner repressions, the worst thing he can possibly do is to try to medicate himself with illicit drugs. There are simply a number of other vastly more effective techniques for helping a person deal with a loss in his overall repressive status. We will be discussing these techniques later in this book.

4.3.2 Drug Abuse as a Symptom of a Psychological Inferiority Complex

Many compulsive drug users suffer from a profound inferiority complex which literally permeates every aspect of their lives. As children, these individuals were generally overwhelmed with negative criticism by their parents. Instead of being told how smart and capable they were, they were repeatedly told that they were stupid and incompetent.[26] Being gullible and overly respectful of the validity of their parents' opinions, these children came to actually believe this negative criticism about themselves. As a consequence, they grew up feeling vastly incapable and incompetent next to the other members of their peer group.

In the beginning, of course, this poor self-image had little or no basis in fact, since virtually all psychologically normal children start out life

---

26. Giving an innocent child a poor self-concept through ruthless criticism is undoubtedly one of the very worst sins an adult can commit, since it contributes to so many problems later on in life.

with their own unique abilities and potentialities. However, as time goes on and a poor self-concept begins to solidify in the mind, the inferior-feeling individual unknowingly begins to act on his poor self-image, i.e. he begins behaving in ways which are consistent with his inferior view of himself. If this process goes on long enough, it can rapidly turn into a case of self-fulfilling prophecy, where the individual creates his own destructive reality out of the negative beliefs he has about himself.

However, it isn't as if such an individual enjoys feeling inferior. He doesn't. In fact, feeling incompetent on a daily basis causes him so much pain that he typically can't bear to face it for what it really is. It is for this reason that the individual with a serious inferiority complex is constantly on the lookout for something which can help to deaden the pain he feels deep inside. Drug abuse is frequently the method of choice for dealing with this inner pain.[27]

Sadly, the chronic abuse of drugs is one of the quickest methods an individual can use to transform the inner belief of inferiority into the actual reality of inferior achievement. For once he starts using drugs to escape the pain of feeling inadequate, he inadvertently starts a self-destructive process into motion which typically won't end until his entire life has been ruined by his drug habit. When this finally occurs, it is usually seen as being the ultimate proof that his parents were right about him all along.

The truth of the matter is that his parents weren't right at all, no matter how much he destroyed his life with drugs. If anything, they were dead wrong. It was his own self-concept which turned out to be "right," because his self-destructive behavior literally forced it to become actualized in the real world. In point of fact he was no less competent than anyone else; he just thought he was incompetent, so he lived his life in accordance with this poor self-concept and created a chronically under-achieving life for himself. Such is the incredible power of self-fulfilling prophecy in a person's life.

However, no matter how much of his life he may have lost to drugs, it is almost never too late for the inferior-feeling individual to redeem himself. Such an act of self-redemption can take place in two related ways: (1) through a radical change in his self-concept; and (2) through an appropriate change in his subsequent behavior. If these two goals can be

---

27. Getting involved in an addictive romantic relationship is another popular way of dealing with the pain of feeling inadequate.

achieved, a person's life can be turned around in a remarkably short period of time.

One of the most profound facts of life is that human beings tend to become what they believe about themselves. The Bible has been telling us this for centuries, but only recently have behavioral scientists begun to realize its true impact. This is why it is so important for us to be positive and encouraging with everyone we come into contact with, especially children: because how we deal with other people directly affects how they feel about themselves, which in turn directly affects what they accomplish in life.

It is sad thing indeed when a person doesn't even come close to approaching his true potential in life. It is as if he has broken one of life's most serious commandments: that of making the most of whatever talents and abilities one has been given.[28] The pain that this realization can cause is unrivaled by any other and can easily lead to suicide if it is not handled properly. Such a crushing response is easy to understand; after all, what good is life if you can't realize your true abilities?

The fact of the matter is that we're here on this earth to grow and develop towards an ultimate version of ourselves which still lies far in the future. As the humanistic psychologists have repeatedly told us, this desire for self-actualization is our deepest need and, as such, it is built into our innermost being. Consequently, when we fail to realize our true abilities, we fail to grow, and when we fail to grow, we fail to fulfill our deepest purpose in being alive. No wonder the inferior-feeling individual feels so horrible inside: he intuitively realizes that he is transgressing life's greatest commandment and that he is negating his own self in the process. No wonder he feels so compelled to use drugs on a daily basis—because the relentless pain of self-negation is so utterly intense.[29]

Fortunately, though, it's almost never too late to change. For as long as a person is still alive there is always time for him to be reborn into a new attitude and self-concept. This is why we need to constantly work with such individuals: because persistence eventually pays off in the transformation of human souls, and turning lives around in this manner is one of the most important things we can do in this world.

---

28. For an interesting discussion regarding the importance of self-actualization in the ultimate scheme of things, please refer to Jesus' Parable of the Talents in the New Testament.

29. Self-negation in this manner is actually a form of psychospiritual death, because part of the personality is getting suffocated on a daily basis. This is why self-negation hurts so bad—because it is being produced by a spiritual substance which is routinely being choked to death.

The key to saving this type of inferior-feeling individual lies in convincing him that the image he has of himself is completely and unequivocably WRONG. Such an individual needs to realize that he is just as talented in his own way as the next person but that his own personal gift just may not have revealed itself yet. Indeed, he needs to realize that his failure to blossom is probably his own fault, since his self-destructive behavior naturally acts to suffocate whatever native talent he does have before it has a chance to take hold and grow. Moreover, he needs to understand that human beings are creatures of belief, in the sense that people automatically become what they believe to be true about themselves. Finally, he needs to understand that he is actually insulting the Great Creator of the Universe by believing himself to be so inferior; after all, why would a Good and All-Powerful God create something that was inherently inferior or unimportant?

Indeed, this tendency for self-deprecation is one of the most tragic consequences of Godless evolutionary theory in the world today.[30] For by convincing millions of people that they are merely the result of a blind and meaningless cosmic accident, Godless evolutionary theory furthers the belief that we humans are unimportant in the ultimate scheme of things. Even worse, it leads people to believe that there are many intrinsically inferior people in the world, because according to the doctrine of Natural Selection, only the fittest people are able to survive.[31] This of course automatically means that inferior individuals naturally die off because of their inherent inferiority.

However, we must be careful to not be deceived. Actual inferiority in human beings is only a relative trait; it can never be considered to be an absolute trait, because all human beings are a vast mixture of all kinds of traits, some of which are inferior when compared to others and some of which are not. Thus, whereas a given individual may be inferior when it comes to muscular strength, he may be superior in some other characteristic, such as overall intelligence. The point is that all individuals

---

30. I use the term "Godless evolutionary theory" to denote the atheistic theory of evolution which is currently being taught in our nation's schools and colleges. It is to be distinguished from what I call "Evolutionary Creationism," which is the belief that God used certain evolutionary processes in His creation of the world. Thus, the true issue here isn't whether evolution actually occurred or not but whether God directed it or not. For a more detailed discussion of this fascinating subject, please refer to my book *Evolutionary Creationism*.

31. Although Natural Selection, or the Survival of the Fittest, is a scientific fact to a certain extent, it doesn't necessarily mean that it was solely responsible for the creation of us all, nor does it necessarily mean that there are intrinsically inferior people in the world.

have both superior characteristics and inferior characteristics when they
are compared with one another. All individuals have some type of
miraculous talent or gift inside of them that no other person can match;
it may be hidden in many people, but it is still there nonetheless. The
existence of the idiot savant, or autistic genius, proves this point once
and for all. Although such an individual may be vastly inferior when it
comes to living an independent life in the outside world, they are
ferociously superior when it comes to their own unique talent, which
may be the ability to memorize phone books or to instantly perform
complex mathematical calculations in their minds.

What these individuals teach us is that all human beings are intrinsically
important and worthwhile, no matter how "inferior" they may seem at a
given task, because all possess some type of superior talent or ability
(which of course is still latent in many individuals). This is why a belief
in God is so important to developing human beings: because it furthers
the belief that we were specially created as the spiritual children of the
Most High God and are therefore important and worthwhile in His
Eyes. This is why it is so difficult for a person who sincerely believes in
God to have a crippling inferiority complex: because he automatically
believes himself to be the creative product of the Greatest Power in all
the universe.

In other words, it is the secular nature of our society in general—and
Godless evolutionary theory in particular—which must bear much of
the responsibility for causing the current drug and alcohol epidemic in
our nation. For by encouraging the belief that human beings are the
result of a meaningless cosmic accident—and are therefore ultimately no
more important than a fish or a rock—it inadvertently helps to instill a
deep inferiority complex in many people, which is often reinforced by
parental criticism and career failure. This inferiority complex in turn
causes people so much pain that they feel driven to abuse drugs and
alcohol in order to get rid of it.

There's no doubt about it. People have a fundamental need to feel that
they are special and important—both in the Universal Scheme of Things
and in their own families—because feeling that one is important leads to
a positive belief in oneself, which in turn motivates the individual to
behave in such a way as to make good things happen in his life. Godless
evolutionary theory acts to oppose this fundamental human need for
feeling special by putting human beings on the same level as fish and

bacteria; no wonder more people than ever before are feeling bad about themselves!

From this perspective it is clear that drug use is only a symptom of a much deeper psychological problem in many people: that of a lack of psychological wholeness, a lack of self-confidence, and a severe deficiency in the ego's self-attained identity structure. In these cases, treating the addiction alone is ultimately self-defeating, because the original psychological problems are left intact. Thus, the best way to treat a pathologically motivated addiction is by first treating the underlying psychological problems which initially gave rise to it. Once this is done, the addiction will usually take care of itself.

Interestingly enough, though, excessive drug use by weak personality types can ultimately prove to be a beneficial thing, since it can direct the attention of family, friends, and the abuser himself to the inner psychological problems which initially gave rise to the addiction. Since it is necessary to first be aware of a problem before one can set about correcting it, it logically follows that anything which makes one's problem more visible can turn out to be a good thing in the long run, but only if the person acts on this knowledge and tries to solve his inner problems with all the power at his disposal.

Unfortunately, though, there are many personality types which are so weak that they don't have the strength or the courage to begin trying to solve their own inner problems. These are the most addicted and hence the most abnormal drug users of all: they are the ones who end up using drugs their entire lives to run away from their problems; they are the ones whose lives are quietly and effectively ruined by their drug use.

4.3.3 The True Nature of Addiction

Now is a good time to discuss the underlying nature of the addictive process. It is commonly believed that one can only become addicted to a psychologically or physically addicting drug, but such is not the case. Addictiveness in general refers to the process whereby individuals who feel inadequate deep inside look for fulfillment in something outside of themselves. When they find it, they rapidly become addicted to it because their psychological well-being depends on it.

According to this definition, just about anything can be desired in an addictive sort of way. For instance, we all know people who are addicted to their work. From a scientific point of view, being addicted to work means having one's inner sense of emptiness and inadequacy negated by one's job. This is why workaholics can't stay away from their jobs for very long: because their psychological well-being depends on their working long hours.

However, perhaps the most popular object of addiction is the romantic partner. Millions of people every year choose to deal with their inner sense of emptiness and inadequacy by falling in love with another person. When this occurs, though, the individual becomes just as addicted to the love object as the heroin addict is to his drug. Proof of this type of romantic addiction is seen when addicted lovers are forced to separate from one another: they go through a type of emotional withdrawal which rivals the withdrawal syndromes of some of the hardest addicting drugs known! I for one would rather withdraw from just about any addictive drug than from a heavily entrenched romantic relationship!

Addictiveness in general is unhealthy, because nothing outside ourselves is truly capable of alleviating the sense of emptiness and inadequacy we have deep inside. We get ourselves into trouble when we insist on disregarding this fundamental truth of life by looking for fulfillment where it cannot be obtained.

The unhealthiness which is generated by the addictive process is caused by three related factors: (1) the pain and frustration of continually fighting a losing battle; (2) the inherent destructiveness of demanding something from the addictive object that it cannot provide; and (3) the lack of developmental progress which results from our misguided search for personal fulfillment. It is as if the addicted individual were looking for food and water in a barren desert on a daily basis; as long as he insists on doing so he is bound to remain hungry, thirsty, and extremely frustrated until death itself intervenes. In the same way, as long as we insist on looking for our fulfillment in drugs or other people—instead of in ourselves—we are bound to remain frustrated and emotionally desolate forever. Indeed, it is a profound spiritual law which can only be broken at one's own peril.

Of course, this isn't to say that it is unhealthy to seek happiness in a personal relationship. It obviously isn't. What is unhealthy is when we try to derive a sense of inner wholeness or completeness from drugs or other people, because no drug or person can ever give this completeness to us.[32]

---

32. True happiness in an interpersonal relationship can only occur between two self-sufficient individuals who don't need each other as a compensation for each partner's lack of inner development. Genuine happiness on an interpersonal basis is thus to be distinguished from the addictive need of someone else for one's own inner stability and self-fulfillment.

There is only one place where true fulfillment can be found and this is inside our innermost selves, in the religious quest for self-knowledge and self-development.[33] The reason for this is simple: the pain and emptiness we feel in our innermost being is actually the result of our not being fully grown on the inside, i.e. our personalities haven't yet grown to full psychospiritual maturity, so the resultant lack of development causes us to feel empty deep inside. It is literally as if a part of ourselves is missing. However, no outside individual or object can give this missing development to us—we need to obtain it for ourselves. Even so, it is still much easier to look for our fulfill-ment in other things and other people than it is to look for it in our-selves. This is why there are so many more addicted people in our society than there are self-fulfilled people!

Interestingly enough, it is the inherent addictiveness of our basic personality structure (and not an inevitable biochemical effect per se) which appears to determine how much we suffer when a lengthy medical treat-ment with narcotics is suddenly discontinued. Studies have shown that people with non-addictive personalities hardly experience any withdrawal symptoms at all when their drugs are discontinued, even if they have been on daily morphine shots for several weeks! On the other hand, individuals with addictive personalities tend to experience a significant degree of withdrawal discomfort after only a brief period of narcotic therapy.

The reason for this intriguing relationship between addictiveness and withdrawal discomfort apparently has something to do with the function of a narcotic in a given personality. In addiction-prone personalities, narcotics generally function to help suppress unwanted thoughts and feelings; hence, when the drugs are withdrawn there is inevitably some type of rebound effect. It is this rebound effect which probably causes the unpleasant withdrawal syndrome. In non-addictive personalities, on the other hand, narcotics aren't generally used to help suppress unwanted thoughts and feelings; they are only used to kill pain. Consequently, there is no rebound effect when the drugs are withdrawn, and hence there is little or no unpleasant withdrawal syndrome. As surprising as it may seem, then, an individual's personality appears to be more influen-tial in determining the extent of addiction than any purely biochemical effect that a given drug may have on the brain.

---

33. This is what religion is all about: self-knowledge and self-development. God wants us to develop our innermost characters as much as possible, because it is only in so doing that we will ever be fit for entry into the future Kingdom of God.

4.4 The Deceptive Lure of Drug Abuse

In many cases illicit drug use is like an evil psychological fixative cement. It appears as though it can be used to repair the inner psychological damage that one has incurred from childhood, but of course, it only turns out to be a quick fix which causes more problems than it solves.

There's no doubt about it: when you play with drugs you are playing with fire. But if this is so true, then why is it that so many chronic users will vehemently deny the dangers of drug use? The reason, of course, is that they are totally brainwashed by their drug habit into believing that drugs are good for them instead of bad. This is the manner in which drugs can have an evil effect on people: they can cause the user to believe that they are actually good for him—that is, of course, until it is too late. THIS is when the true evil of drug use finally shows itself: when the chronically abusing person finally realizes that he has been brainwashed by his drug habit for twenty or thirty years, and that he has lost his entire life in the process.

This is why the serpent in the Garden of Eden was so evil: because he appeared to be so good. In the same way, extensive drug use is also evil, because it appears to be a good thing. Some of the very worst evils in life are undoubtedly those which go around masquerading as good.

On the other hand, it is quite possible to use certain drugs recreationally from time to time with virtually no ill effects whatsoever, except for perhaps a slightly depressed immune system. Such a person could hold a responsible position in society and be a perfectly good spouse and parent. In fact, there are literally millions of responsible people in this country who use drugs and alcohol from time to time in a recreational fashion without ever encountering major problems—unlike the chronic, heavy drug abuser.

Nevertheless, it is hard to tell whether even such miniscule use will ultimately turn out to have a negative effect on the user. Who's to say whether or not these people would have been happier or more productive had they not ever consumed any type of psychoactive drug at all? To be sure, it fits the pattern of the deceptive evil of drugs to note that they don't appear to be negatively affecting one's life until it is too late. The recreational drug user might be functioning well in his day-to-day life, but who is to say whether or not he would be functioning better if he stayed straight all the time?

Chapter 5

THE EFFECTS AND HAZARDS OF DRUG ABUSE

While the initial effects of drug use can be extremely pleasant, the potential hazards of using are equally real and foreboding, as we have already seen. Indeed, the use of the word "potential" here is something of a misnomer, since virtually all drug users will experience something hazardous sooner or later.

In this chapter we will catalog the major effects and hazards of the various classes of psychoactive drugs, including both prescription and non-prescription drugs.

5.1 Marijuana

Marijuana is comprised of the ground up leaves and flowertops of the weed Cannabis sativa. The active ingredient is the mild hallucinogen tetrahydrocannabinol (THC), although there are over 400 other chemicals contained in the smoke. It also goes by the following slang names: pot, reefer, resin, grass, herb, number, doobie, sinse, stuff, and weed.

The most potent form of marijuana is called hashish, which is the concentrated resin from the plant's flowertops (2%–4% THC). It is much more potent than ordinary marijuana and usually costs about $10 a gram. Hash oil is the THC-rich oil (up to 30% THC) which is extracted from hashish and usually costs around $100 for a tiny bottle. It is typically applied to the outer paper of cigarettes, so it can be consumed in a rather inconspicuous fashion.

Interestingly enough, the strains of marijuana which are commonly available now contain an average of 4% THC by weight; this is over ten times the potency of the strains which were available just a few short years ago, which averaged only 0.4% THC. Indeed, a highly cultivated form of marijuana called Sinsimilla contains as much as 7% THC and can easily cost $250 to $300 an ounce. This is how much a whole pound was selling for back in the middle seventies!

Thai-sticks are another popular form of marijuana. Made of marijuana from Thailand which has supposedly been dipped in opium, it is wrapped around a stick and sold for anywhere between $25 and $50 a stick. It is extremely potent and can cause a profound intoxication in even the most experienced of users.

Different types of marijuana seem to offer their own unique sort of high, in much the same way that different wines and liquors provide their own unique sort of intoxication. For example, "Red Bud" Columbian strains give the user a heavily drugged, "downer" sort of feeling, whereas "Maui Waui" strains from Hawaii give the user a much more cosmic, ethereal sort of high. This is why most marijuana connoisseurs like to keep as many different types of marijuana on hand as possible: so that they can choose the type of high that they want on any given day.

Most forms of marijuana are smoked in ordinary pipes, joints (self-rolled cigarettes) and water pipes (bongs). Regardless of the manner in which it is consumed, the smoke is typically drawn deep into the lungs and held there for an extended period of time, in order to maximize absorption. In fact, when a "hit" of marijuana is held in the lungs for around a minute or so, the smoke actually disappears, so that virtually nothing is exhaled. This is due to the fact that it is almost completely absorbed by the body in that amount of time.

Recently, the pharmaceutical industry has introduced the first legal form of marijuana to the American public, a pill whose generic name is dronabinol (brand name Marinol). Used primarily for the treatment of nausea in cancer chemotherapy patients, it has virtually all the effects of regular marijuana, since it contains marijuana's primary active ingredient, delta-9-THC. It has also been used to treat high intraocular pressure (glaucoma).

5.1.1 Effects

What happens when a person lights up a joint and gets high? Although different people experience getting high in different ways, most users go through a distinct series of events when they "cop a buzz."

First, a person may cough as he seeks to hold a "hit" of smoke in his lungs as long as possible in order to maximize the effect. This coughing then slowly gives rise to a feeling of light-headedness and well-being. If the conditions are right he soon may become overwhelmed by a sense of general hilarity; everything suddenly seems unbelievably funny, regardless of how ordinary and pedestrian it may actually be.

A pot smoker will also usually experience subtle changes in his thinking and sensory abilities when he is on the drug. More often than not, he will find that his higher faculties have become greatly compromised and that his lower senses appear to have become enhanced, i.e. whereas he may no longer be able to think very critically on marijuana, he may find that his lower senses are enhanced: music seems to sound better and food seems to taste better.[34]

In fact, it is a common experience after getting high to get "the munchies," where you suddenly are famished and feel like eating all sorts of different foods, especially sweets. Often getting high will also cause "cotton mouth," an unpleasant state where your mouth is so dry that you find it uncomfortable to even talk. This, of course, is relieved by consuming lots of fluids.

During the entire experience of being high a person typically begins to get progressively enveloped by a general sense of lassitude, which in a few hours usually gives way to a drug-induced lethargy or sleep. This is the state of "crashing" from the high that so many people repeatedly experience, which results from the drug actually leaving the brain cells.

As far as other side effects are concerned, a marijuana intoxication can cause any of the following: bloodshot eyes, dizziness, perceptual difficulties, confused thinking, irritability, poor coordination, depression, overall weakness, sluggishness, loss of muscle tone, hallucinations, headache, depersonalization, unsteadiness, disorientation, tachycardia (rapid heart beat), paranoia, anxiety and loss of memory.

Paranoid reactions in particular are especially troublesome for many chronic marijuana users. When these paranoid thoughts occur, users tend to suspect that the police or some other type of "uncool" individual is watching them or following them. Although the majority of these paranoid reactions center around the legitimate fear of getting caught, they can sometimes grow so far out of proportion to any realistic fear that they make normal life impossible. Indeed, legendary guitarist Carlos Santana is reported to have given up marijuana smoking a long time ago because of his paranoid reactions to the drug.

Anxiety reactions to marijuana smoking are also relatively common. In certain individuals this reaction can be so severe that prompt medical attention is required to avert a serious psychological catastrophe. Indeed,

---

34. The reason marijuana seems to cause a heightening of one's sensory abilities appears to be related to its ability to reduce the repressive load that the mind is constantly laboring under. Such a decrease in repressive ability liberates a certain amount of neurological energy which then can be sublimated into a feeling of enhanced perceptile ability. Of course, the flip side to this weakening of repression is that it can also cause the unwanted thoughts and feelings residing in the unconscious to rise to conscious awareness.

thousands of emergency room visits relating to marijuana use are reported each and every year all over the country.

Marijuana smokers also have a notoriously poor memory, both when they are intoxicated and when they are relatively "straight." It is quite common for them to stop talking in midsentence because they actually forget what they are trying to say. This effect largely goes away when they quit smoking for good, but in some people the poor memory persists indefinitely. Such a decrease in tolerance to the effects of marijuana smoking occurs after several closely spaced highs. When this occurs, a person typically needs to consume more and more of the drug in order to regain the original high. For this reason, some users allow a significant amount of time to pass between each use of the drug. Others compensate for this "burned-out" effect by consuming stronger and stronger varieties of marijuana, or by consuming a good deal more of the drug each successive time they get high.

This is why there is truth to the idea that pot leads to stronger drugs. For while there is nothing intrinsic to marijuana which inevitably leads the user to stronger drugs, the very fact that each successive marijuana "buzz" typically gets less and less intense makes it more likely that other drugs will be resorted to in the search for the perfect high. Indeed, for many people the very use of marijuana has the effect of breaking the drug-abusing "ice"; since they are already using one illicit drug, it suddenly isn't that big a deal to "graduate" to another, more powerful one.

A final interesting effect of pot smoking concerns how one sees the world while high. In many people, pot appears to provide a much more external and detached view of the current reality at hand. That is to say, many pot smokers feel like part of their conscious mind is able to leave their bodies while high, so that they can go to a much more all-encompassing perspective, usually that of being on the ceiling looking down. This phenomenon allows the pot smoker to grasp a totally different understanding of the particular events at hand. For some people, however, this new perspective can be downright frightening and intimidating.

5.1.2 Hazards

Contrary to popular belief, marijuana isn't the totally harmless drug most users think it is. All sorts of health risks are associated with marijuana smoking; they just seem to be negligible when compared to the dangers of heroin and cocaine. Indeed, the widespread belief among pot smokers that marijuana is harmless only adds to the sinister quality of the drug. For by convincing themselves that it is so harmless, they continue using it and never realize the harm that's happening to them until it's too late.

Marijuana can precipitate all sorts of health problems in the chronic user. For one thing, it alters the natural course of psychological development in children and teenagers, so it can have devastating psychological effects when its use is begun at an early age. These effects range from severe immaturity and dependence in adolescence and adulthood to the development of the famous "amotivational syndrome," where the user doesn't feel motivated to do much of anything but eat, laugh, and sleep! It can also greatly compromise the student's intellectual ability, which often causes him or her to perform at a level far below his own native ability. Most frightening of all, it can trigger panic reactions in susceptible people and can even bring on psychotic episodes in those who are predisposed to them.

Although most marijuana users don't display such severe symptomatology, a good deal of subtle harm can still be gradually taking place below the surface of things. There's no doubt about it. Marijuana is an *extremely* insidious drug. It weaves its way into the inner fabric of a person's psychological life by binding with his very own brain cells, and in so doing it can cause significant changes to his personality, sometimes forevermore. However, since it is so widely believed that marijuana is a relatively harmless drug, millions of people continue to use it day after day.

There is nothing worse than a potentially harmful stimulus which no one believes is actually harmful. After all, if something is obviously dangerous, we are naturally forced to respect its power over us; on the other hand, if something is not overtly dangerous and is even believed to be safe, we are much more likely to use it on a daily and even an hourly basis, and this greatly magnifies any harmful effect it could be having on us.

As far as the physical risks of marijuana use are concerned, the major risk appears to be the damaging of lung tissue. It has been shown that marijuana smoke contains 70 percent more benzopyrene, a profoundly carcinogenic chemical, than cigarette smoke does. And since marijuana smoke is typically held in the lungs for the longest possible time in order to maximize absorption, this can increase the risk of cancer in the chronic user. (It still hasn't been absolutely proven whether or not marijuana smoking is more carcinogenic than cigarette smoking.)

In fact, benzopyrene is such a powerful cancer-causing agent that when it is sparingly applied to the shaved skin of mice, skin cancers typically result within a day or two! Now I don't know about you, but I don't want to be holding any benzopyrene deep within my lungs for any extended period of time!

The latest research out of the Duke University Medical Center has shown that chronic marijuana users also suffer from dramatically lowered blood flow to the brain. Using state-of-the-art brain imaging techniques, Doctor Roy Matthew and his associates were able to demonstrate that chronic users of at least ten joints a week for a minimum of three years had greatly lowered cerebral blood flow patterns when compared to straight controls.

According to Doctor Matthew, normal brain blood flow and brain function are closely coupled; the more brain blood flow, the greater the overall brain functioning capacity will be. Marijuana users, on the other hand, typically have a lowered brain functioning capacity, which shows itself in lethargy, memory deficits, and a slower overall reflex time. This decreased brain functioning capacity thus seems to be directly related to the lower amount of blood flow to the brain that marijuana causes.

It is a well-known fact that the brain is by far the most sensitive organ in the body to a decrease in overall blood flow. This is why the brain has the best supply of newly oxygenated blood branching off the aorta; it is also why brain blood flow and overall brain functioning capacity are so closely related. Moreover, a reduced amount of brain blood flow is known to induce all types of brain function deficits, ranging from psychotic reactions and memory problems to panic attacks and mood changes. Thus, by decreasing the overall amount of blood flow to the brain, chronic marijuana users are probably greatly reducing the overall functioning capacity of their brains; they are also probably making themselves more susceptible to various psychiatric problems as well.

It doesn't make much sense to try to feel good by deliberately reducing the amount of blood flow to the most sensitive organ in your body. It's like trying to improve the performance of a sports car by deliberately reducing its horsepower! Feeling good naturally requires an optimal amount of blood flow to the brain. This is one of the main reasons why long-distance runners experience "runner's high" so often: because running greatly increases the overall amount of blood flow to the brain. This increased blood flow naturally increases the amount of oxygen and other vital nutrients which end up reaching the "feel good" center of the brain, which in turn greatly increases its capacity to feel euphoric. Chronic marijuana users, on the other hand, routinely starve their brains of these vital nutrients by decreasing their overall brain blood flow with marijuana. No wonder chronic marijuana users are so lethargic and listless: they are inadvertently suffocating their brains into relative inactivity with their pot smoking!

Marijuana has also been shown to have a slight depressive effect on the body's immune system. Although such a slight depression may not seem to be very significant, it could easily turn out to be the critical difference between health and disease. After all, with the hundreds of thousands of new toxins which have been introduced into our environment over the last several decades, our immune systems are having to struggle more now than ever before. The last thing any of us need is even a slightly compromised immune system, because such a weakening can make us more susceptible to cancer, various autoimmune disorders, and even the AIDS virus.

As far as marijuana's effects on the male reproductive system are concerned, several studies have linked chronic marijuana use to lower testosterone (male sex hormone) levels. However, these lower levels were shown to be reversible upon extended abstention from the drug.

Other studies have documented an inverse correlation between male sperm count and marijuana use; as marijuana use goes up, the sperm count goes down. Similar studies have further shown that some of the sperm from daily pot smokers are deformed and non-functional. Consequently, any male whose wife is trying to conceive or who has borderline endocrine function should definitely not be smoking pot.

As far as the female reproductive system is concerned, a recent study found that women who had been smoking marijuana for at least 6 months had abnormal menstrual cycles three times as frequently as a control group of non-users. These abnormal cycles were related either to a failure to ovulate or a decreased overall period of fertility. These findings suggest that marijuana use may decrease fertility in women.

Marijuana use has also been shown to have an adverse effect on pregnancy. THC-treated monkeys, for example, were shown to be four times more likely of having an aborted or stillborn baby than a control group of non-treated monkeys. Moreover, males born to these THC-treated monkeys had a lower-than-normal birth weight. It has also been demonstrated in the laboratory that THC is contained in mother's milk and can therefore be transmitted to a nursing baby. Consequently, on the basis of these experimental findings, it is only flirting with disaster to smoke marijuana while you are pregnant or nursing.

While marijuana has never been conclusively shown to cause brain damage, one recent experiment with rhesus monkeys who were trained to smoke a single joint five days a week for six months showed lasting changes in the microstructure of their brain cells. And while we have no absolute proof that the same thing happens in humans, the odds are very high that it does, since human brains and monkey brains are neurologically much more similar than we like to think.

Other studies have shown that chronic marijuana use can widen the space between brain cells. And since brain cells communicate with each other by sending chemicals called neurotransmitters across this space, called a synapse, a wider space can mean a longer time to communicate a particular message. This alleged phenomenon correlates well with the much slower cognitive reaction time that can typically be seen in chronic marijuana intoxication. It also correlates well with the severe memory deficits which are routinely seen in chronic pot smokers. Perhaps the synapse is so disturbed by the presence of the drug that some of the neurotransmitters which are released never make it to the other side in an intact fashion. This would appear to cause instant forgetting, something which is seen all the time in pot smokers.

As far as marijuana's effects on the heart are concerned, it is a well-known fact that a few puffs from a joint can increase heart rate by up to 50 percent. This can have tragic consequences in those with heart problems. It can bring on angina (chest pain) attacks, stimulate fatal arrhythmias, and even bring on an incipient heart attack. Consequently, anyone with heart problems should completely avoid the use of marijuana.

For years it was assumed that marijuana was unable to cause physical withdrawal symptoms since it was believed that marijuana was not physically addicting. However, with the advent of pharmaceutically pure forms of marijuana (dronabinol pills), it has been learned that there are indeed both physical and psychological withdrawal symptoms when a person tries to kick a rather extensive marijuana habit. These withdrawal symptoms include restlessness, irritability, and sleeplessness, and can set in as soon as 12 hours after the drug has been discontinued. A day after the drug has been withdrawn, hot flashes, a stuffy nose, loose stools, sweating, loss of appetite, and hiccups may take place. These bona fide withdrawal symptoms will usually dissipate rapidly after 3 or 4 days. However, if a user undertakes the treatment program discussed in the next chapter, he could very easily avoid suffering any withdrawal symptoms at all.

5.2 LSD and Other Hallucinogens

Lysergic acid diethylamide, or LSD, is a synthetic hallucinogen which was discovered by the legendary chemist Albert Hoffman in his laboratory at home. It has since been the subject of millions of conversations and the cause of millions of drug-induced psychedelic "trips."

LSD reached the height of its popularity during the late sixties and early seventies. Doctor Timothy Leary of Harvard did a great deal to promote the use of LSD with his admonition that we "tune in, turn on, and drop out." Indeed, LSD was even used by a good many psychiatrists in an attempt to bring new levels of insight and understanding to their patients.

It wasn't long, though, until the bad effects of LSD began to present themselves to the nation. Hundreds of LSD-inspired drug casualties began to make the headlines almost every day. More and more people began to have bad experiences while on LSD, and for a significant percentage of them, these bad experiences didn't go away when the drug's effects finally wore off. LSD was blamed for causing a rash of suicides, with Art Linkletter's daughter being one of the most famous.

Today, LSD isn't nearly as popular as it was a couple of decades ago, largely because of the bad reputation it has received in many drug-using circles. Another reason for the decline of LSD's popularity over the years is undoubtedly the move to political conservatism in this country. LSD is a drug of the radical left, and since many of our young people now are much more conservative in their outlook on life, it is only natural that they are abandoning the use of LSD in favor of such conservative-type drugs as alcohol and cocaine.

5.2.1 Effects and Hazards

LSD exerts its main effect by interfering with the neurochemistry of serotonin in the brain. This biochemical alteration causes subjective effects which can range all the way from a sense of hilarity and expanded awareness to frank hallucinations and an outright psychosis.[35]

LSD causes such a totally all-encompassing experience that its users call it "tripping." This is a reference to the extended "trip" you take in your mind while on LSD. Such an experience usually entails a profound

---

35. Serotonin is an inhibitory neurotransmitter which is intimately involved with the process of repression in the mind. When this inhibitory substance is itself inhibited with LSD, the serotonin-mediated "repressive lid" which caps the unconscious mind is partially lifted. It is this partial liberation of the mind's unconscious contents which causes the extreme mental and emotional changes which are routinely seen in LSD intoxication.

alteration in a person's perspective and attitude towards life. Indeed, since LSD causes such a profound reshuffling of one's internal cognitive landscape, many people have utterly terrifying reactions to the drug. This is what "bad trips" are all about.

Few people realize how tenuous our psychological grip on normality can be; for some all it takes is a relatively intense chemical or experiential stressor to trigger an emotional breakdown. This is because of the repressed "volcano" of emotional pain which lies inside most of us just below the level of conscious awareness. All it takes for this emotional volcano to "erupt" is some form of extreme stress in our lives. LSD is more than strong enough to elicit this reaction. Indeed, this is a primary reason why so many people have had extended psychotic reactions to the use of LSD: because the drug precipitated the release of a disturbance which already existed as a distinct potentiality inside of them.

Because of this devilish ability to precipitate serious mental illness in its users, suicide is the greatest hazard associated with the use of LSD (with serious mental illness running a close second). Of course, these suicides aren't necessarily intentional. Indeed, a great many people on LSD have inadvertently killed themselves because they believed they could fly or do some other dangerous or impossible thing.

LSD also has the frightening ability to cause "flashbacks" in people, sometimes years after their last experience with the drug. During a flashback you suddenly re-experience an LSD trip in all of its original intensity. Since it comes out of nowhere (often at the most inopportune of times), it can be an extremely frightening experience indeed.

Any drug which interferes with brain function at such a fundamental level is bound to be dangerous, if not in the present, then in the future. Sure, LSD has been known to provide the most rapturous experiences imaginable, but it has also been known to provide the most hellish experiences imaginable as well. And since you never know whether you're going to end up in a chemically induced heaven or hell, the only intelligent thing to do is to not take it at all and to get your pleasure in more natural ways. Certainly life is full of immensely pleasurable experiences; all we need to do is to take full advantage of them instead of relying on a miserable pill to do the "pleasing" for us.

There is something which is fundamentally wrong about trying to seek pleasure in a pill. It is though we were trying to bypass or short-circuit the natural path to pleasure which God Himself gave us. The natural domain of pleasure is in the arena of our external behaviors and in our internal reactions to them; when we attempt to cheat this natural system by resorting to self-stimulation with powerful brain-altering chemicals, only pain and misery can ultimately result.

5.3 Cocaine

Cocaine is a pharmaceutical derivative of the South American coca plant. The local peasants of the Andean highlands in South America have chewed coca leaves for thousands of years without much ill effect, due to their relatively weak potency. However, once modern man learned how to extract the active ingredient from the plant, he soon became prey to the profoundly addictive power of pure cocaine.[36]

Cocaine has an interesting history behind it. Sigmund Freud, one of the founding fathers of modern psychology, fell in love with the drug after trying it a few times. Impressed by its stunning ability to eradicate depression and invigorate its users, Freud began to enthusiastically give the drug to his friends and family. However, soon thereafter the demonic, health-destroying powers of the drug rapidly began to present themselves, so Freud quickly gave up on the seeming wonder drug.

At one time the soft drink Coca-Cola had cocaine as one of its major ingredients. This is why it was called Coca-Cola: because it contained ingredients from the coca plant and the cola bean; it is also why Coke used to pack such a powerful punch! But when it was learned that cocaine was so addicting, they removed it from the Coca-Cola formula and replaced it with caffeine.

Cocaine is often used in medicine as an anesthetic, but it is its stimulant properties which have made it so popular in the drug-using subculture.

Cocaine can be purchased on the street in two major forms: powdered cocaine hydrochloride, which sells for about $100 a gram, and crack, which is a much more potent form of cocaine that sells for between $10 and $20 for a tiny piece of the poison. The reason crack seems so inexpensive when compared to cocaine is that it is sold in much smaller quantities, but since you end up using more, it costs you much more in the long run.

Crack is a much more potent form of cocaine because it is smokable.

---

36. The organic form of most naturally occurring drugs is almost invariably less damaging than the refined form, due to the weakened potency of the drug and the presence of other alkaloids which help to moderate the drug's effects.

Because it is smoked, it generates an overwhelming high in just a few seconds, as opposed to a couple of minutes with traditional cocaine powder that is "snorted" into the nasal cavity. Tragically, though, crack is much more addicting than the already highly addicting powdered form of cocaine, largely because it leads to such a profoundly intense high, which is soon followed by an equally prodigious low.

5.3.1 Effects

The effects of a cocaine high are both profound and legendary. When a quarter gram or so is "snorted" into the nasal passages, an extremely intense "rush" and overall euphoria is felt soon thereafter. This rapidly gives rise to a profound sense of optimism about the world and one's own place in it. A person could be in the middle of a dungeon and still feel that all is right with the world when he is on cocaine!

This is why cocaine is so addicting: because it is so utterly reinforcing. Evidently, cocaine stimulates the pleasure center of the brain in the most effective manner possible; this is why users are compulsively driven to repeat the experience so often.[37]

Cocaine's other psychological effects include distortions of perspective, delusions of grandeur, extreme mood swings, constricted mental functioning, and feelings of exhilaration and self-confidence. Behavioral effects include hyper-alertness, talkativeness, inability to sleep, reduced sense of humor, heightened sense of self-awareness, altered sexual capacity (low doses tend to enhance sexual ability, while higher doses depress it), repetitive behavior, altered perceptions, and an extreme tendency towards addiction. In fact, according to Doctor Calvin Chatlos, director of the adolescent substance abuse division of Fair Oaks Hospital, 85 percent of users said that they couldn't turn cocaine down when it was offered to them, while more than 75 percent said that using cocaine was preferable to any other activity in life, including eating and having sex!

All in all, a cocaine high is similar to the high you get from speed, in that it appears to sharpen your awareness while simultaneously giving you a sense of unending energy. Thus no matter how tired you may be, a little cocaine seems to bring you back to life, at least for a little while.

This is where the bad part comes in. For just as soon as you realize that you're in "cocaine heaven," you begin to leave it for a much more

---

37. Interestingly enough, a stimulation of the brain's pleasure center also produces a sense of optimism in an individual. Apparently, it is natural to feel optimistic about the world when one is simultaneously feeling great pleasure.

ominous visit to "cocaine hell." Of course, different people react in different ways while coming off of the drug, but a significant percentage of users experience disturbing psychological symptoms while "crashing" from the intense high. These symptoms appear to be due to cocaine's high degree of interference with the brain's own chemical messengers.

As Doctor Chatlos explains in his excellent book *Crack: What You Should Know About the Cocaine Epidemic,* the repeated use of cocaine

> disrupts the delicate balance of three neurotransmitters—norepinephrine (NE), dopamine (DA), and epinephrine (E). These neurotransmitters can have a natural stimulant effect on the brain. Cocaine causes certain brain cells to release their supplies of NE, DA, and E, and this produces the cocaine "rush."
>
> The brain rapidly uses up its reserves of these neurotransmitters. As cocaine use continues, the brain cells are able to release less and less NE, DA, and E. The result is that bigger and bigger doses of cocaine are needed to produce the same effect. This imbalance in directly responsible for many of the negative effects of cocaine: lethargy, anxiety, insomnia, nausea, sweating, and chills.
>
> A person who uses cocaine regularly may not realize just how much trouble he is in until he tries to stop taking the drug. By then, the supplies of NE, DA, and E are so low that the brain doesn't have enough to meet its normal everyday needs. The neurotransmitter-starved brain goes through withdrawal, experiencing effects the opposite of the original cocaine high: depression instead of exhilaration, physical pain instead of euphoria, and so on. Most of all, it desperately craves cocaine.
>
> How powerful is this craving? When laboratory animals are given unlimited access to cocaine, they prefer it to food, sex, literally everything else. They use it until it kills them. (Pp. 18–19.)[38]

To be sure, if one disturbs the incredibly complex biochemistry of the brain with ANY drug, only misery and dysphoria can ultimately result. The brain is only capable of a limited amount of euphoria, simply because its stores of pleasure-stimulating neurotransmitters are so small. Thus, when a person tries to exceed the brain's natural capacity for pleasure with the repeated use of cocaine, he is on the road to trouble.

Some users, however, appear to be able to "crash" from a single high with few bad results. The more often it is used, though, the more likely it is that unpleasant effects will follow the initial high.

---

38. Calvin Chatlos, *Crack: What You Should Know About The Cocaine Epidemic* (New York: Putnam, 1987), p. 20.

However, no matter who the user is, cocaine's major effect is to make you want to do it again and again and again. Some people have enough self-control to limit themselves to only a few highs a month or so, but the majority of users find this degree of self-control almost impossible to muster up. If the supply of cocaine is steady (and even if it isn't), each successive use of the drug makes you want to continue using it that much more. This is where the widely acknowledged evil of the drug comes in. For each time you do the drug the high gets less and less intense, so it takes more and more of the drug to get you as high as you were the first time you took it. This of course leads to all sorts of personal havoc as the drug abuser tries desperately to get enough money to keep his cocaine supply steady. And since even a moderate habit can end up costing several hundred dollars a day, it is no wonder that many cocaine addicts end up dealing drugs, stealing, or prostituting themselves so they can come up with the money to support their habit.

If a person continues to use cocaine, he finds that he suddenly needs to keep taking the drug, not so much to feel euphoric, but just to avoid cocaine's horrible withdrawal symptoms. For once a person gets trapped in the vicious addictive cycle of cocaine, his entire life rapidly becomes subordinated to the drug. All of sudden the addict's schoolwork, job, family, and friends become totally meaningless as he begins to devote his entire life to the acquisition of his poison. Of course, such abject slavery to cocaine can't continue for very long, because eventually most addicts will either lose their physical and mental health or end up getting caught by the police.

It certainly is no accident that experimental animals respond to cocaine in much the same way humans do. The drug is so utterly reinforcing that any creature with the capacity to feel pleasure will seek to use it as much as possible, even if it ends up killing them in the process.

In order to fully appreciate just how addictive cocaine is, consider the following experiments facts: (1) In only 30 days, cocaine-using rats lost up to 47 percent of their body weight, several had seizures, and an incredible 90 percent died outright! (2) Rats who were allowed to have cocaine ignored foot shocks to keep getting the drug. (3) Rats preferred the cocaine bar to the food bar. (4) Male rats ignored a receptive female rat so they could continue pressing the cocaine bar. (5) Monkeys will press a bar for cocaine even if it takes 12,800 presses for a single dose![39]

---

39. Ibid.

It is truly amazing—and frightening—to realize that we humans are so similar to the "lower" animals when it comes to our behavioral response to cocaine. The drug obviously has the power to induce a self-destructive frenzy in any mammal that takes it, including man. *This alone should be reason enough to persuade any half-rational individual to totally avoid the use of cocaine.*

5.3.2 Additional Hazards

All sorts of serious health problems can result from the chronic abuse of cocaine. Repeatedly snorting cocaine into the delicate nasal passages can cause the septum, which separates the two nostrils, to perforate, or develop a hole in it. It can also cause a chronically stuffy nose and severe postnasal drip.

Other physical symptoms associated with cocaine abuse include tachycardia (rapid pulse rate), hypertension (high blood pressure), rapid breathing, elevated body temperature, sweating, dry mouth, dilated pupils, headache, gastric distress (nausea, vomiting, abdominal discomfort), loss of appetite, dehydration, anorexia, hyperglycemia (elevated blood sugar levels), muscle bracing, an urge to evacuate the bladder and/or bowels, and various nutritional deficiencies.

Since smoking crack is a much more potent and systemic method of using cocaine, it can lead to even more serious physical problems than snorting cocaine does. These problems include seizures, chest pain (from decreased blood flow to the heart), heart attacks (through a disruption in the heart's electrical system), poor circulation, bronchitis, tracheitis, heavy coughing and wheezing, loss of voice, asthma attacks, severe bouts of anxiety, and bone-crushing depression.

The use of cocaine reportedly increases the risk of spontaneous abortion in pregnant women, so anyone who even suspects that she may be pregnant should totally abstain from any cocaine use. Because cocaine crosses the placental barrier, the use of cocaine by a pregnant woman will cause the fetus to be addicted as well, and this greatly jeopardizes its normal development and even its very life. Moreover, cocaine can be found in mother's milk, so nursing mothers should also avoid its use.

Cocaine can even kill you if the circumstances are right, regardless of how small a dose is used. Doctor Chatlos describes this tragic phenomenon as the "impossible overdose," which results because some people simply cannot metabolize cocaine properly. Consequently, using cocaine for the first time is like playing Russian Roulette, since even a tiny dose can lead to death if one possesses this problem. According to Doctor Chatlos, a history of breathing problems under general anesthesia or following the use of Anectine, a muscle relaxant, indicates the distinct possibility for such an "impossible overdose."

However, the most frightening problem associated with chronic cocaine abuse (apart from outright death) is the development of a paranoid psychosis which is virtually indistinguishable from the real thing. Only getting withdrawn from the drug for a prolonged period of time can eliminate this problem, and even then a cure isn't guaranteed. The repeated stimulation of the brain by cocaine can precipitate a latent psychosis, such that when it develops, it will most likely remain until long after the drug is withdrawn; it may even last forever.

Richard Pryor apparently suffered a drug-induced psychotic reaction during his repeated bouts of smoking freebase cocaine. In a television interview with Barbara Walters, Pryor explained how freebasing cocaine day after day eventually made him want to kill himself. So in a drug-induced frenzy he decided to burn himself to death using lighter fluid which he squirted all over his body. Fortunately he lived to tell about his terrible ordeal, albeit with severe burns over a large percentage of his body.

Another potential health hazard associated with the use of cocaine is neurological in nature. It has recently been hypothesized that chronic cocaine use can cause the generation of new cocaine receptors in the brain. If this is true, then it stands to reason that the frequent user will feel extremely uncomfortable whenever these newly formed receptors aren't filled with cocaine. Such a prediction correlates well with the evidence: chronic cocaine addicts literally go nuts when they don't have a steady supply of their poison.

But who wants to create new receptors in the brain because of cocaine abuse? The brain's unbelievably complicated neural circuitry is already so complex that scientists will probably never fully understand it, so it makes me shudder to think that chronic cocaine users might actually be growing new receptors in their brains! There is no high in the world which is worth the neurological disfiguring of our precious brain tissue.

Again we come to the same conclusion: the many hazards of cocaine use make it impossible to justify taking it at any time for any reason. Len Bias, the great college basketball star from the University of Maryland, thought he would try crack just once to see what it was like; after all, what possible harm could come from such a single tiny use of cocaine? Well, as you probably remember, the harm was swift and final: the crack interfered with the conduction of electrical impulses in Bias's heart and he dropped dead!

It's true! Even a single dose of cocaine can kill you if the situation is right. With Len Bias and Don Rogers of the Cleveland Browns, the situation was right and now they're gone from this world forever. Was it worth it for them to use cocaine just a single time? Of course not! Len Bias had a great professional basketball career ahead of him. Don Rogers also had a great professional football career ahead of him with the Browns. Tragically, though, he allegedly thought he would try some cocaine during his stag party the night before his wedding, and the rest is history.

We mustn't be so audacious as to think that we've got our bodies and minds totally under control. We don't. The human body is by far the most complicated thing we know of; its biochemical complexity is so deep and far-reaching that scientists have only begun to scratch the surface in trying to understand it. Yet every time we take cocaine, or any other harmful drug, we are interfering with our body's natural chemical processes in ways that none of us can even imagine. So who's to say whether or not a given drug will interrupt our internal biochemistry to the point that severe illness or even death itself will intervene?

Again, we see that it is simply not worth it to use cocaine even a single time for any reason. After all, one time can be all it takes to ruin your life . . . forever. A few minutes of fake pleasure will NEVER be worth the risk of addiction, getting caught, or outright death. To be sure, God did a good enough job in constructing the human brain the way He did; when we try to add to it by ingesting dangerous chemicals, only pain and misery can ultimately result.

5.4 Narcotics

Narcotic drugs include the natural derivatives of the opium poppy plant, such as morphine and codeine, and any of their synthetic analogs, such as heroin and dilaudid. They work by binding with the brain's own natural opiate receptors, and their effects are both profound and legendary.

5.4.1 Effects

The chief therapeutic effect of all narcotic drugs is analgesia, or the relief of pain. Interestingly enough, narcotics don't seem to have any direct effect at all on the physiological source of pain. On the contrary, they simply alter our reaction to pain by disconnecting our awareness from it. Consequently, when a person who is in pain takes narcotic drugs, he no longer suffers as bad; the pain may still be there, but he just doesn't care about it anymore!

However, as far as addicts are concerned, it is the profound euphoria following the use of narcotics which makes them so enticing. This euphoria involves an intensely pleasurable brain and tissue response which literally permeates a person's entire being. Interestingly enough, though, only certain people appear to be prone to these effects; not surprisingly, they are the same people who have addictive personalities.

The other side effects of narcotic use include nausea, vomiting, dizziness, light-headedness, sleepiness, headache, loss of appetite, dry mouth, flushing of the face, constipation, itching of the skin, agitation, lack of coordination, minor hallucinations, disorientation, visual disturbances, tachycardia, palpitations, urinary difficulties, faintness, reduced libido (sexual drive), skin rashes, hypoglycemia (low blood sugar), anemia, yellowing of the skin and/or whites of the eyes, and precipitation of seizures in susceptible people.

The most ominous effect of narcotic use, however, is the rapid development of chemical tolerance upon repeated administration of the drug. Tolerance simply means that the user needs to keep upping his dose in order to recapture his original euphoria. This of course leads to the rapid escalation of use which is routinely seen in severe cases of addiction.

5.4.2 Hazards

Death—either intended or unintended—is a very real possibility with narcotic abuse, since an overdose can quickly lead to respiratory collapse. Heroin addicts in particular are in danger whenever they get a new supply of their poison, because they can never be sure of the potency of their new supply. If it is much more potent than their previous supply, using the same dose can rapidly lead to respiratory collapse and sudden death. Fortunately, if an overdosing addict can be caught in time, the depressant effects of narcotics can be reversed with the use of nalorphine, a narcotic antagonist.

Although all narcotic drugs can be exceedingly dangerous, a particular word of warning is in order for propoxyphene (Darvon) abusers. Darvon is a chemical derivative of methadone, a potent narcotic. However, because Darvon is among the weakest of the semi-synthetic narcotic analgesics (being only two-thirds the potency of codeine and about as effective an analgesic as aspirin), many assume that it is a relatively safe drug to abuse. Nothing could be farther from the truth.

The fact of the matter is that Darvon has a profound sedative effect in high doses which is far greater than its limited analgesic power (this sedative effect is multiplied even further if alcohol is consumed). Thus, if a relatively non-tolerant individual were to take a large enough dose of Darvon or were to combine it with alcohol, death could easily ensue.

Indeed, Darvon is one of the few drugs which carries a special boxed-in warning in the *Physician's Desk Reference* (PDR). This warning specifies that Darvon should not be prescribed to suicidal or addiction-prone individuals or to those who tend to abuse alcohol. Most importantly, the PDR reports that sudden death can result in as quickly as fifteen minutes if a sufficient dose of Darvon is taken.

At one time the chief health risks associated with narcotic addiction were malnutrition, collapsed veins, and a severely compromised immune system. These days, however, the biggest risk involves catching the deadly AIDS virus from the sharing of hypodermic needles. However, this genuine danger can be totally avoided by using only sterile needles and by not sharing them with anyone else.

Since I.V. drug users constitute the second largest population of AIDS victims, we should be providing them with sterile needles free of charge. While this may seem to condone their drug use, it is a sacrifice we need to make if we are to make any significant headway into curbing the spread of the deadly AIDS virus in our society. After all, serious users are going to inject their poison whether we give them sterile needles or not. However, since these users threaten us all when they spread the AIDS virus, we should be protecting ourselves by giving them sterile needles without second thought.

5.5 Barbiturates

Barbiturates make up a sizable percentage of the sedatives and sleeping pills which are routinely prescribed in this country. They are also used to help control seizures in epileptics. They function by disrupting certain nerve channels in the brain.

Barbiturates are known as "downers" in the drug-using subculture. They include secobarbital (Seconal), phenobarbital (Luminal), amobarbital (Amytal), pentobarbital (Nembutal), and butabarbital (Butalan). These compounds differ primarily in their potency and their duration of action. Although methaqualone (Quaalude, Parest) isn't made from barbituric acid, its effects are remarkably similar to those of the barbiturates.

5.5.1 Effects

The chief effect of the barbiturates is that of progressive sedation, depending of course on the dose. Many people liken a barbiturate intoxication to being drunk on alcohol; indeed, drinking on top of barbiturates can lead to greatly increased sedation and even death, due to the profound amount of synergism between the two drugs (which means that the effects are much greater than additive).

Side effects of the barbiturates include drowsiness, difficulty in breathing, rash, lethargy, dizziness, nausea, vomiting, diarrhea, hangover, anemia, and yellowing of the skin.

The barbiturates don't offer the intense euphoria that cocaine and narcotics do. They simply calm anxiety and make one feel drunk. However, the barbiturate-like compound methaqualone (Quaalude, Parest) does give the user a pleasant sense of euphoria; this is why they were so popular among recreational users. In fact, Quaaludes were so totally abused back in the seventies that the drug companies were eventually forced to quit making them entirely! Now the only Quaaludes which are available are the "bootleg" versions which are made in illicit laboratories.

5.5.2 Hazards

The chief hazard associated with barbiturate use is the risk of sudden death from either impaired driving ability or outright suicide. Barbiturates can greatly impair a person's ability to operate heavy machinery as well, especially if alcohol is also simultaneously consumed.

Barbiturates have the distinction of being the drug most commonly used for drug-induced suicides. It is even possible to inadvertently commit suicide with barbiturates, due to their ability to severely cloud consciousness. A person can lose track of how many pills he's taken over the course of a day or night and keep taking more until death from respiratory collapse eventually ensues. Drinking alcohol at the same time greatly potentiates the drug's effects and so vastly reduces the number of pills that can safely be taken.

Overall, an oral dose of 1,000 milligrams of most barbiturates causes severe poisoning in a full-sized adult. Death occurs after an oral dose of between 2,000 and 10,000 milligrams. This relatively narrow margin of safety makes barbiturates exceedingly dangerous, since only 20 pills can kill a person, and even less is required if a person has been drinking!

Barbiturates are also known to suppress REM sleep, which is the stage of sleep where dreaming occurs. When they're taken for just a few days at a time this suppression of dreaming doesn't cause much of a problem.

But when they're taken for weeks at a time, a serious cumulative effect is typically seen, such that when the drugs are finally discontinued, a terrible rebound effect generally occurs, which can lead to extensive nightmares and even daytime hallucinations. Indeed, if this drug-induced suppression of dreaming continues long enough, a person can begin having these terrible break-through symptoms while still on the drug. The brain clearly has a need for nightly dreaming, so that when REM sleep is artificially suppressed with drugs, a very bad reaction is bound to occur.

Barbiturates are also strongly suspected of causing fetal injury in pregnant females. Moreover, definite withdrawal symptoms are seen in infants who are born to mothers who have regularly used barbiturates during the last trimester of pregnancy. Consequently, pregnant women should totally avoid the use of any of the barbiturates.

Finally, because the barbiturates are so physically addicting, withdrawing from an extensive habit can be extremely difficult, and even fatal if it is not properly managed. Withdrawal symptoms include overwhelming anxiety, intolerable agitation, muscle twitching, tremor of hands and fingers, weakness, nausea, vomiting, dizziness, profuse sweating, delirium, confusion, inability to sleep, and sudden grand mal seizures. These symptoms begin to set in approximately eight to twelve hours after the last dose and continue over a period of approximately fifteen days. Because these symptoms are so potentially dangerous, it is best to seek professional help when trying to kick a deeply ingrained habit.

5.6 Tranquilizers

There are two main classes of tranquilizers: the major tranquilizers (such as Thorazine and Mellaril) and the minor tranquilizers (such as Valium and Librium). The major tranquilizers are used for their sedative and antipsychotic effects in severely disturbed people, while the minor tranquilizers are mostly used for treating anxiety in otherwise normal people.

The major tranquilizers have almost no propensity at all for abuse, since they don't generate euphoria in the user. On the contrary, they make most people feel absolutely terrible; some have even likened their effects to that of a "chemical straightjacket."

The minor tranquilizers, on the other hand, are much more likely to be abused, due to their ability to reduce anxiety down to tolerable levels.

This is why they are so psychologically addicting: because it is easier to depend on these drugs for help in getting through the day than it is to deal directly with the stress in one's life. Unfortunately, though, the minor tranquilizers are also physically addicting as well. Indeed, as the experiences of Betty Ford and others have shown us, trying to kick a substantial tranquilizer habit can be one of the most harrowing experiences in life.

5.6.1 Effects

The primary effect of the major tranquilizers is sedation without sleep (although large doses can easily have a hypnotic effect). In psychotic patients with thought disturbances, the major tranquilizers apparently have the ability to help normalize their thought patterns.

It was the large-scale use of the major tranquilizers in mental hospitals back in the fifties which helped to send tens of thousands of otherwise untreatable patients back home again. Although these drugs don't even come close to providing a cure for deep-seated mental problems, they do help to make patients more manageable.

The primary effect of the minor tranquilizers is the quelling of anxiety. They are used to help control the withdrawal symptoms of acute alcoholism and to help people cope with the common, everyday stresses of life.

5.6.2 Hazards

There are some very real hazards which are associated with chronic use of the major tranquilizers. Jaundice, liver injury, motor restlessness, pseudo-parkinsonism, hypotension, endocrine disorders, skin pigmentation, ocular changes, cerebral edema, photosensitivity, and paradoxical psychotic states are just a few of the side effects which are seen with varying frequency in patients who are using these drugs. In fact, almost an entire page of the *Physician's Desk Reference* is devoted to the many side effects that these powerful drugs can cause!

Accidents can also easily happen while one is taking a major tranquilizer, due to the depressant effect it has on the central nervous system. Fortunately, however, it is quite difficult to commit suicide with any of these drugs, although a coma can be induced with a large enough dose.

Undoubtedly, though, the most serious potential side effect of chronic "therapy" with the major tranquilizers is persistent tardive dyskinesia, a horrible condition which is characterized by rhythmical, involuntary movements of the face, tongue, mouth, and jaw. At times these movements may also be accompanied by involuntary movements of the extremities. Frighteningly enough, there is no known treatment for this syndrome (although it has been reported that high-dose manganese therapy is extremely effective for some people). Apparently these drugs permanently damage a critical part of the brain which is associated with these movements.

A more subtle hazard involves the profound suppression of a person's inner potential for growth and success when he is on chronic "therapy" with these tranquilizers. Since these drugs prevent you from being your true self, they also prevent you from utilizing your true potential in life. This of course is a tremendous evil, especially when one considers the fact that these drugs are not curative in any sense of the word.

Most psychiatrists prescribe these drugs because they are at a loss to help their patients in any other way. However, putting a defenseless psychiatric patient in a "chemical straightjacket" doesn't really qualify as help at all most of the time. On the contrary, for all but the most difficult of cases, it is a tragic life sentence, with the doctor condemning the patient's true personality to a lifetime of involuntary incarceration within the prison of a chemical lobotomy. This is a hideous crime against humanity and so should be avoided as much as possible.

Worst of all is the fact that most psychiatric patients trust their doctors to the end, and so they blindly take whatever "medication" is given to them under the assumption that it is in their own best interest. But how can a chemically stifled pseudo-life be in the patient's best interest? In all but the most severe of cases, it can't be. On the contrary, it is usually in the doctor's own self-interest, because it gives him an illusion of competency and makes him less responsible for the patient's well-being; after all, it is easier for most psychiatrists to blame the patient for his incurability than to take the blame themselves for not knowing what to do. Giving psychiatric patients personality-destroying drugs is also in the self-interest of the psychiatric institution as well, since it makes these patients much more docile and hence renders them a good deal easier to manage.

At any rate, although the major tranquilizers are not physically addicting in the traditional sense, they do cause a profound change in one's state of mind. Consequently, when they are withdrawn a definite psychological withdrawal syndrome can often be noted. This syndrome is largely due to the spontaneous reorganization of the mind's cerebral contents and is characterized by profound changes in a person's attitude and perception of reality. Many have likened it to the lifting of a veil of fog from around the mind.

As far as the minor tranquilizers are concerned, their primary hazards center around their great susceptibility for abuse. These drugs are both psychologically and physically addicting, so they need to taken with a certain amount of respect and responsibility.

A withdrawal syndrome which is similar in kind to barbiturate withdrawal, though usually of less intensity, occurs upon termination of a minor tranquilizer after repeated use. However, certain psychological effects can be even more severe, such as paranoia and confusion. The bottom line, of course, is that you can't chemically suppress anxiety for weeks and months at a time without having a vicious rebound of the anxiety when you finally quit taking the drug.

Although large doses of the minor tranquilizers can have profound hypnotic effects, it is relatively difficult to commit suicide with them. This is extremely fortunate, since a certain percentage of the people who are prescribed these drugs are the same ones who are likely to be considering suicide.

Like barbiturates, these drugs can also greatly depress the central nervous system, so accidents are more likely to occur when a person is on them. Consequently, one should avoid driving a car or operating dangerous machinery while taking these medications.

Other less serious side effects associated with minor tranquilizer use include drowsiness, fatigue, constipation, confusion, double vision, headache, hypotension, incontinence, jaundice, urinary retention, changes in libido, slurred speech, skin rash, nausea, blurred vision, and paradoxical anxiety reactions.

5.7 Amphetamines

Amphetamines (uppers, bennies, dexies, speed) are central nervous system stimulants. They are particularly popular among college students and truck drivers, who use them for their ability to keep them awake and alert for extended periods of time. They are also popular with dieters because of their ability to suppress appetite.

5.7.1 Effects

The primary effect of the amphetamines is stimulation of the central nervous system, which usually makes the user feel good. It also helps to lift a depressed person's mood (at least temporarily) and tends to make him feel more optimistic about the world and his own place in it. This effect is remarkably similar to the mood-lifting effect of cocaine and is undoubtedly related to the fact that both drugs are CNS stimulants.

The CNS stimulation brought on by amphetamines has several therapeutic uses. For instance, it is used to treat narcolepsy, a bizarre disease where one suddenly and uncontrollably falls asleep right in the middle of a daytime activity. This of course can be extremely dangerous, especially if you are driving a car. Amphetamines act to counter this sudden tendency to sleep by stimulating the nervous system to a higher overall level of alertness.

Amphetamines are also to treat hyperactivity in children. This paradoxical effect results from the fact that hyperactive children are already maximally stimulated from within. Thus, when they are given a drug which further stimulates them, they can't get any more stimulated, so they calm down. This is known as the "inverted-U phenomenon," which simply means that if you are stimulated while already experiencing maximal stimulation, there is nowhere else to go but down.

Amphetamines also are said to stimulate an area of the brain known as the "red nucleus," which acts to filter the amount of information reaching conscious awareness. In many hyperactive children the filtering ability of the red nucleus is underutilized; this allows a flurry of unfiltered neural impulses to reach conscious awareness, which in turn distracts hyperactive children to the point that their overall attention span is greatly shortened; this is why they are so hyperactive. Stimulating the filtering ability of the red nucleus with amphetamines thus has the effect of reducing the overall amount of stimulation reaching conscious awareness, which in turn increases the attention span and reduces the overall hyperkinesis.

The use of amphetamines (including Ritalin, a non-amphetamine stimulant) to treat childhood hyperkinetic syndrome has become extremely controversial in recent years. Many people are appalled by the use of powerful drugs to treat a problem whose ultimate cause appears to lie elsewhere, and rightly so, because the only sensible way to treat a medical problem is by eliminating the cause of the problem, not by treating symptoms alone with drugs. But since the cause of most hyperactivity syndromes is to be found in the child's diet, environmental exposures, or his relationship with his parents, most physicians find it much easier to prescribe drugs to treat symptoms than to find and treat the true cause of the problem. This is bad medicine, because it harms the child in both a physical and a psychological way.

Ritalin in particular has had a devastating psychological effect on many children. Not only is it an extremely addicting drug, it also seems to cause supreme havoc in the psychic equilibrium of many children, and this only helps to confirm the negative psychiatric labelling which has been applied to them. How long is it going to take the medical establishment to realize that toxic chemicals are rarely, if ever, the best way to treat a given behavioral problem?

Amphetamines are also used as short-term appetite suppressants in dieters. However, this use of amphetamines is also bad medicine, since the true cause of most cases of obesity lies in faulty life-style patterns. Thus, if the patient doesn't alter his life-style by eating better foods and by exercising every day, the fat which was lost with the aid of amphetamines will come back just as soon as the drugs are discontinued.

5.7.2 Hazards

The side effects of amphetamine use include palpitations, restlessness, overstimulation, dizziness, insomnia, hypertension (high blood pressure), tachycardia (fast pulse), hallucinations, muscle spasms, headache, dry mouth, constipation, diarrhea, itching, decreased libido (sex drive), and psychotic reactions.

Amphetamines are also known to cause birth defects, so it is extremely unwise to use them during pregnancy or nursing.

However, the primary hazard surrounding the use of amphetamines is their high tendency for abuse. Any drug which makes you feel as good as amphetamines do is bound to be abused. Like all shortcuts to euphoria, though, they can quickly get you into trouble if you're not careful.

As with cocaine, the repeated use of amphetamines rapidly causes a severe depletion of neurotransmitter levels in the brain. This of course leads to an extremely unpleasant withdrawal syndrome when the drug is discontinued, which is characterized by profound fatigue and depression, coupled with an intolerable craving for the drug.

But it isn't as if the only problems associated with amphetamine abuse occur when the addict's supply runs out. On the contrary, the repeated stimulation of the brain by amphetamines can quickly lead to a paranoid psychosis that is virtually indistinguishable from the real thing. Many users also begin to feel a severe sense of itching below the surface of their skin after prolonged use, which they liken to bugs crawling around inside of them. In their drug-induced frenzy, they have been known to scratch deep gashes in their skin to help alleviate the itching.

It was precisely these horrible effects which led to the phrase "Speed Kills" back in the mid-sixties. Indeed, there appears to be no way to reach a happy medium with amphetamine abuse: you get into trouble if you continue using the drug, and you get into trouble if you run out of the drug. Consequently, if you've never taken amphetamines before, you should probably leave well enough alone and not try them. If you're addicted to them, though, the best thing to do is to get off of them as soon as possible.

5.8 Nicotine

Most people don't consider nicotine a drug, but the fact of the matter is that it is one of the most hazardous drugs that money can buy. In fact, nicotine kills more people every year than all other drugs combined! That's right, cigarette smoking kills more people every year than crack, heroin, and alcohol (including drunk-driving accidents) put together! This is truly an incredible statistic, but it serves to remind us how two-faced our society really is: we spend millions of dollars fighting international drug trafficking when the most dangerous drug of all is freely available at any corner gas station!

Pharmaceutically speaking, nicotine is equally deadly: a single purified drop of this potent nerve poison can cause instant death through a paralysis of the nervous system! This is why nicotine is often included in various insecticide formulas: because of its ability to paralyze the nervous systems of insects.

But if nicotine is so profoundly dangerous, then why do most people not consider it a drug? There are three basic reasons: (1) it doesn't cause an intoxication, (2) it's legal, and (3) it only kills after it has been used for a number of years (drugs like crack and heroin, on the other hand, can kill you in a few seconds).

5.8.1 Effects

The primary effect of nicotine on the body is vasoconstriction and a mild stimulation of the central nervous system. Nicotine also seems to have a suppressive effect on emotions; the very act of drawing the poisonous smoke deep into one's lungs seems to help push unwanted emotions out of conscious awareness.

People quickly become tolerant to many of nicotine's subjective effects, so that they continue to smoke or chew, not in order to attain any positive effects, but just out of habit and of course to keep any unpleasant withdrawal symptoms at bay.

5.8.2 Hazards

There are two primary ways of ingesting nicotine: in the form of cigarettes and in the form of chewing tobacco or snuff. Either way can cause big problems for the user.

The hazards of cigarette smoking are so widely known that they hardly need mentioning here. Virtually every serious disease in the book is either brought on or made worse by smoking. Heart disease, stroke, emphysema, and cancer all are directly related to cigarette smoking, as are birth defects, premature deliveries, and low birth-weight babies. In fact, Surgeon General C. Everett Koop has called cigarette smoking "the chief preventable cause of death in our society and the most important public health issue of our time."

The many horrible diseases which are induced by smoking are undoubtedly caused by the multitude of poisonous chemicals which are contained in cigarette smoke. Carbon monoxide, cyanide, benzopyrene, and a thousand and one other serious poisons are contained in the deadly smoke. With this in mind, it isn't at all surprising that cigarettes are so deadly; what is surprising is that so many people are able to remain relatively healthy while smoking on a daily basis![40]

Many people are beginning to use chewing tobacco and snuff in response to a media blitz extolling the benefits of going smokeless. Unfortunately, though, this route of administration can be just as hazardous to the user as smoking can be.

The chief hazard associated with chewing tobacco and snuff is oral cancer. In fact, approximately 10 percent of all oral cancers are currently being blamed on smokeless tobacco. Studies have shown that women who have used snuff for a long period of time have four times the chance of developing oral cancer that non-users have; for women who have used snuff over fifty years, the risk jumps to an astounding fifty times normal!

But it isn't as if it always takes decades for oral cancer to develop. For some people, all it takes is a few short years before a deadly cancer results from the repeated use of snuff or chewing tobacco. Take the case of nineteen-year-old track star Sean Marsee, for example. Sean began dipping snuff when he was twelve years old. A malignancy on his tongue showed up six years later, and nine months after that he was dead.

Although Sean's mother repeatedly warned him about the dangers of using snuff, Sean continued to use it anyway, because he was convinced that if it really was dangerous, the tobacco companies would have already

---

40. Being able to simultaneously smoke and be healthy is definitely a temporary phenomenon. Sooner or later, the vast majority of cigarette smokers are going to pay dearly for their deadly habit.

put warning labels on the cannisters. As a consequence, Sean's mother has filed a $37 million lawsuit against the U.S. Tobacco Company for their willful negligence. She correctly claims that the tobacco company knew full well how dangerous their product was and so should have put a warning label on the package.

Other health risks associated with smokeless tobacco include gum recession, periodontal disease, tooth wear, and leukoplakia, which is an unsightly callous in the mouth that is considered to be pre-cancerous.

The use of smokeless tobacco has now reached near epidemic proportions, with anywhere between 7 and 22 million people using the product daily. What is even more tragic is the fact that children and teenagers make up a large percentage of these users. Indeed, one study showed that 28 percent of high school age boys in Massachusetts reported some use of smokeless tobacco. In some rural Texas and West Virginia towns, it has been estimated that between 50–75 percent of all school-age boys "rub Skoal."

The cancer-causing chemicals in smokeless tobacco are called nitrosamines. They are ten times more prevalent in snuff than in chewing tobacco and about one thousand times more prevalent than the amount found in bacon. Although nitrosamines are extremely carcinogenic, there is a type of nutritional antidote which can help to counteract the effects of these poisons. It has been known for some time that ascorbic acid (vitamin C) can detoxify the nitrosamines, thereby rendering them non-carcinogenic.[41] Consequently, it makes sense to take several vitamin C tablets a day if you continue to chew tobacco or rub Skoal.

5.9 Inhalants

The inhalants include those volatile chemicals which are inhaled for their intoxicating effects. They include gasoline, spray paint, paint thinner, transmission fluid, White-Out, various aerosols, model airplane glue, nitrous oxide, and butyl nitrate.

5.9.1 Effects and Hazards

The effects obtained from inhaling any of the toxic chemicals listed above vary from substance to substance. All of them are capable of causing a near-immediate "high," dizziness, headache, nausea, vomiting,

---

41. This is why vitamin C is often added to ham and bacon: so that the carcinogenic nitrites they often contain as preservatives (which turn into nitrosamines in the body) can be detoxified.

and loss of consciousness. The more serious effects of long-term usage include the development of an organic brain syndrome, which is characterized by confusion, irritability, lethargy, psychosis, loss of coordination, and disorientation. Other serious side effects include peripheral nerve damage and liver and kidney disease.

Many of the compounds which are sniffed for "pleasure" are known carcinogens, so there is also a greatly increased chance of developing cancer in chronic abusers. Gasoline, for example, contains benzene, an exceedingly poisonous compound which is known to cause leukemia and anemia after repeated exposure.

The most serious hazard, though, from inhaling these volatile substances is outright death from heart failure or respiratory collapse. In fact, in 1978 over 150 people died as the direct result of inhaling these poisons with the intention of getting high.

What is so surprising about inhalant abuse is that the "high" one gets from them is vastly inferior to the highs that one can get elsewhere, even from alcohol. And considering the severe health damage that inevitably occurs in response to chronic use, only a self-destructive fool would continue using them. To be sure, even heroin addiction is a good deal less damaging to one's overall health than the inhalants are.

5.10 Alcohol

Ethyl alcohol is by far the most widely used intoxicant in this country. It is also the most widely abused intoxicant as well, with over 20 million people currently classified as alcoholics and millions more suffering in one way or another from their excessive drinking.

5.10.1 Effects

The effects of an alcohol intoxication are quite familiar to most people. With small doses, alcohol consumption tends to reduce a person's inhibitions, thereby facilitating social interaction and leading to a perceived good time. Small doses also have an anti-anxiety effect, which helps millions of people unwind every evening after a hard day at work.

With larger doses one begins to see a progressive impairment of motor and intellectual functioning, along with slurred speech, drowsiness, muscular incoordination, and extreme dizziness (the spins), which is when the room you are in appears to be spinning around relentlessly. If a person continues to drink, he soon loses consciousness altogether.

5.10.2 Hazards

The chief hazard associated with alcohol intoxication is death by accident. Indeed, tens of thousands of people inadvertently lose their lives every year in alcohol-induced tragedies. Fully half of all automobile accidents involve alcohol as a primary cause, and 33 percent of all accidents and crimes are said to be linked to the use of alcohol.

It is even possible to drink oneself to death outright. Gulping (chugging) an entire fifth of Scotch all at once, for example, will kill all but the most hardy of souls. Unfortunately, such a tragedy happens almost every year as naive teenagers race to see who can finish a bottle of whiskey the quickest.

There are many other hazards which are associated with alcohol abuse. Tens of thousands of divorces every year are caused largely by chronic alcoholism. Countless other families are forced to endure all manner of hardship as one or both parents slowly drink themselves to death.

Of course, chronic alcoholism can cause cirrhosis of the liver, a well-known, progressive disease where the liver is slowly destroyed by alcohol-induced scar tissue. Chronic alcoholism can also cause severe malnutrition, mental illness, death of brain cells, and greatly decreased productivity.

Ethyl alcohol is a profoundly addicting drug. Once a person is hooked, only a truly monumental effort will free him from his habit. Indeed, the withdrawal syndrome associated with a deep addiction to alcohol is one of the most frightening experiences known to man. The worst part of this withdrawal process is undoubtedly the condition known as "delirium tremens" (or the "DT's"), where one goes into a horrible mental delirium which is characterized by a severe trembling of the hands and feet. If the condition isn't properly treated, it can result in outright death.

Fortunately, though, the terrors of withdrawal can largely be avoided by modern methods of detoxification. Consequently, anyone trying to kick an extensive addiction to alcohol should check into a professional detoxification ward as soon as possible. To be sure, there is no need to suffer so intensely if you don't have to. (Ironically, though, suffering a great deal during withdrawal can have the beneficial effect of persuading a person to never go back on the bottle again, no matter what.)

All in all, in terms of the overall amount of suffering involved, alcohol is far and away the most destructive intoxicant in our society. Nothing else even comes close.[42] Marijuana, for example, isn't even 1 percent as

---

42. In terms of overall disease and mortality, nicotine is the most destructive non-intoxicating drug in our society.

destructive; yet the DEA spends millions upon millions of dollars chasing pot smugglers while almost totally ignoring the tragic effects of alcohol. Our society clearly has a double standard when it comes to drug and alcohol abuse, but this open hypocrisy must cease if we are to ever make any significant headway into combating the drug problem.

Chapter 6

MORE ON THE HAZARDS OF DRUG ABUSE

There are a great many additional hazards associated with drug abuse over and above those directly caused by the drug's biochemical effects on the body. In this chapter we will discuss the most important of these hazards.

6.1 The Retarding of Development in School-Age Children

One of the most subtle hazards associated with drug abuse involves the retarding of psychosocial development in school-age children. It is a subtle hazard because it is hard to tell what a particular child would have been like had he or she never begun using drugs, i.e. it is hard to distinguish between the drug's effects and the child's own native personality.

The fact of the matter is, though, that chronic drug abuse by growing children has the effect of hiding their true, non-drugged personalities from both themselves and the rest of the world during the single most important time of their life. This can lead to a severe identity crisis later in their development, since these veteran drug abusers typically have no idea about who they really are or what they're actually like off of drugs.

In other words, drug abuse by school-age children can severely alter the normal developmental process, thus rendering the children more immature and less in control of their lives than they ever would have been otherwise; it can also greatly compromise their overall level of intellectual functioning. Normal psychological development requires the child to grow through certain critical non-drugged stages on the way to adulthood. If these stages are bypassed or cut short because of drug abuse, then the child's normal psychological development will be altered and some sort of problem will eventually result.

This phenomenon of altered development due to drug abuse can be compared to the process of creating a vase with wet clay. If the vase is to be formed properly, only pure clay must be used. If the clay is adulterated with a severe weakening agent, the final product will be much weaker and less durable than it would have been otherwise.

Similarly, if potent psychoactive drugs are mixed into the personality structure as the child is growing up, the final product is bound to be weaker and less durable in one way or another.

Nevertheless, there are still some people who begin using drugs in elementary school and then go on to become successful and productive in their adult years, no matter how many drugs they consume. But these people are definitely in the minority, and they probably are still damaged by their drug use in one way or another.

The point of all this, of course, is that it is infinitely preferable to keep children off of all drugs if possible, because it is during the critical childhood years that the personality grows most rapidly. If drugs are to be used at all in life, it is best to wait until one has reached full psychological adulthood, so that the normal course of one's development won't be compromised as extensively.

6.2 Suicide

One of the greatest risks associated with the abuse of drugs is depression-induced suicide. Just about any psychoactive drug can cause a severe depression if it is abused enough, and when there is depression, there is always the risk of suicide. In fact, drug abuse is one of the early warning symptoms of a potential suicide.

In March of 1987 we had a tragic reminder of the relationship between drug abuse and suicide. Four teenagers suffocated themselves to death with automobile exhaust after using cocaine not long before. Of course, we don't know whether the cocaine actually caused the suicides or whether it was simply used as a final mind-altering ritual. Either way, though, the cocaine didn't help matters any; if anything, it probably contributed to the suicides by making the kids more depressed and by clouding their minds to the point that they were able to perform such a self-destructive act.

A common misconception regarding suicide is that talking about it makes it more likely to happen. This is hogwash. The fact of the matter is that not talking about it makes it more likely to occur. So if either you or someone you know is contemplating suicide, don't be afraid to talk about it, because doing so often helps to dispel the urge to do away with oneself. If there is no one else to talk to, call up your local suicide prevention center or simply dial 911.

The most important thing to realize about suicidal feelings is that they are almost always temporary, especially if they are in response to a bout of drug abuse. If the individual contemplating suicide can just hold out for a few more days, these suicidal feelings will usually leave just as quickly as they came. Few problems in life are truly insoluble, and even the ones that are (such as terminal cancer) don't warrant "treatment" by suicide.

We are here to learn and grow in life. But since we often learn and grow the most in response to painful stimuli, we need to learn to endure whatever suffering comes our way. We do not learn or grow by committing suicide.

Interestingly enough, most potential suicides don't really want to kill themselves at all; they want something else, such as health, a romantic partner, or happiness in general. Consequently, when they feel like they'll never be able to get what they really want, they go ahead and kill themselves. However, nothing is so important in life that the loss of it warrants the taking of one's own life. Unfortunately, though, while in the throes of depression few people are able to think so critically.

6.3 Drug Abuse as Deception

From time immemorial the notion of evil has been associated with deception. Beginning with the Garden of Eden, the greatest evils in life have been those which are able to deceive us the most, because they cause us to base our behavior on beliefs which are totally false. As a direct consequence of these false beliefs, we end up committing all sorts of destructive behaviors.

According to this definition of evil, drug abuse is one of the greatest evils known to man because it is so utterly deceptive. Users are routinely deceived into believing that drug abuse isn't so bad and that what they're experiencing with drugs is true pleasure. Because these beliefs are false, however, they become more and more enslaved by their drug habit, which in turn leads them to engage in all manner of destructive behavior.

Clearly, if the extreme destructiveness of drug abuse is to be avoided, a way must be found to expose the false beliefs which are naturally engendered by it. For if the user can be persuaded that drug abuse is really dangerous and that it doesn't provide true pleasure, he is MUCH less likely to continue using drugs.

In other words, the best way to reduce drug abuse in this country is through effective user education, since it is only through education that the false beliefs engendered by drugs can be debunked forever. Once these false beliefs are destroyed, the rational user will no longer want to use drugs again.

6.3.1 The Illusion of Drug-Induced Pleasure

As we noted above, there are two primary deceptions which promote drug abuse: the belief that drugs aren't so bad and the belief that they cause true pleasure. Actually, most users are familiar with the destructive effects of drug abuse, but they are still persuaded to use drugs anyway because of the seemingly wonderful highs they get from them.

In other words, as far as the drug abuser is concerned, the end justifies the means: the end of drug-induced euphoria justifies whatever destructive means it takes to get there. Consequently, if we could somehow reduce the pleasure that users get from drugs (or at least think they get from them), we could greatly increase their incentive to stop on their own. One of the best ways of doing this is by convincing them that drug-induced pleasure is actually a weak counterfeit of its true real-world counterpart.

The fact of the matter is that drug-induced pleasure is an illusion, pure and simple; it doesn't even qualify as being a genuine pleasure in any authentic sense of the word. Sure, many drugs are capable of inducing a profound euphoria in the user, but this feeling is just that—a feeling, a sensation. It isn't an authentic, real-world experience, because the user isn't actually doing anything in the external world to naturally elicit such a pleasurable sensation; he is simply taking a biochemical shortcut to pleasure by artificially plugging up certain brain receptors with drugs.

Such an experience doesn't constitute true pleasure at all. On the contrary, genuine pleasure can be defined as a natural internal response to a pleasurable real-world behavior that you are engaging in. (In the case of meditation, pleasure is a natural internal response to an internal, non-drug behavior one is engaging in.) With drug abuse, the biochemical responsiveness of the brain is divorced from the real-world experience of the whole person; instead of feeling pleasure in response to a legitimate real-world experience, the drug abuser bypasses this experience altogether by going straight to the brain's own pleasure receptors. Such a practice is not only unnatural, it is downright dangerous as well, for the brain was designed to experience pleasure only when it flows out of a natural response to a real-world experience. Bypassing this natural progression with drugs throws the whole system out of whack and opens up a frightening Pandora's box of evil consequences.

The point here is that the brain is only capable of a certain amount of biochemical pleasure in a finite amount of time, approximately equal to the maximum amount of pleasure a person can get at one time from a real-world experience. When this amount is exceeded with drug use, a sort of "pleasure debt" is rapidly created within the brain's neurotransmitter system. It is the "repayment" of this debt which produces the suffering that a user experiences when he goes without his drugs.

In other words, the only pleasure the human brain was designed to experience is the kind that the brain initiates itself in response to a real-world behavior. Any attempt to forcefully short-circuit this natural cerebral response artificially with drugs creates problems, just as short-circuiting a computer inevitably causes it to malfunction.

The upshot of this discussion is straightforward and to the point: what seems like pleasure to the drug user isn't really true pleasure at all—it is just a biochemical, organismic sensation based on false premises.

Interestingly enough, the ability to experience real-world pleasure varies from individual to individual. Some people are capable of experiencing great pleasure (or at least what seems to be great pleasure) on a daily basis, while others experience pleasure much more infrequently. Indeed, depending on the extent to which a person's internal development has been blocked by accumulated psychopathology from the past, it is possible that he or she may be totally unable to experience any pleasure at all in life. In psychiatry this is called anhedonia, and it usually results from a mind that has defended itself so much against experiencing its own pain from the past that it is unable to open itself up to the possibility of pleasure in the present. Chronic drug abuse, especially of narcotics and other sedatives, is often a primary symptom of this inner defensiveness against unconscious pain.

To be sure, when feelings have been routinely deadened for a lifetime in an attempt to avoid the feeling of old childhood pain, real-world pleasure in the present is bound to be a casualty as well. In order to be able to feel pleasure you have to be able to feel pain; thus, if you routinely block painful feelings, you simultaneously block pleasurable feelings at the same time.

Unfortunately, though, most of us have been repressing old painful feelings from our past ever since childhood. In so doing, we have simultaneously repressed our ability to experience true pleasure in the present. Consequently, it seems that if we are to ever be able to experience the maximal amount of pleasure of which human beings are capable, we must first purge ourselves of our accumulated unconscious pains and childhood hangups.

Given the amount of pleasure that we as a repressed people are able to experience, it truly makes me shudder to think about the degree of pleasure we will be capable of experiencing once we have done away with our repressions once and for all! The joy and ecstasy that we will experience just at the thought of being alive will vastly exceed any type of "pleasure" that can be obtained from a mere drug. Surely, this is what St. Paul had in mind when he predicted that

> Eye hath not seen, nor ear heard, neither have entered into the heart of man, the things which God hath prepared for them that love him (1 Cor. 2:9, KJV).

Few people realize that the Biblical goals of sanctification and purity of heart are actually religious synonyms for self-actualization and unrepression, respectively. We are here on this earth to forge a unique and independent psychospiritual identity for ourselves; once this is accomplished, we will then be qualified to take up residence in the heavenly Kingdom to come. Psychologists have called this developmental goal for man self-actualization or individuation, but it is actually what the Bible has meant by the term sanctification all along. In order to be sanctified or made whole, though, we must first purify our heart (i.e. mind) by purging ourselves of all our accumulated repressions, for it is only in so doing that we can feel genuine pleasure and continue growing in our lives. God wants us to feel the most pleasure of which we are capable, so He repeatedly urges us in the Bible to "purify our hearts" of our accumulated repressions—because He knows that it is the only way that we will be able to experience the true joy of unrepressed pleasure.

6.3.2 Drugs and Sex

It never ceases to amaze me how many drug users think they are enhancing their sexual lives by taking drugs. In point of fact, nothing could be further from the truth. After all, most psychoactive drugs alter sensation by anesthetizing or deadening the nervous system, and you can't fully feel a given sensation when your body is anesthetized! Certain drugs such as alcohol may lessen one's cerebral inhibitions, but they still end up deadening one's physical sensations just the same. Indeed, many lifelong drug users go through their entire lives never having experienced the true pleasure of sex, because they have insisted on anesthetizing themselves everytime they have sex with drugs.

There's no doubt about it. Being straight is the only way to experience the true pleasure of sex—or for that matter, the true pleasure of anything. Because you are fully awake and in total control of your senses when you are straight, you can fully appreciate the entire spectrum of whatever pleasurable activity you are engaging in. With drug-induced pseudo-pleasure, on the other hand, a person's consciousness is usually so constricted that he is only able to notice a small percentage of the actual pleasure at hand.

For instance, if one is especially turned on by music, getting "way into" a favorite song will provide a much more authentic and lasting pleasure than any mere sensation that a foreign chemical can give. In fact, studies have shown that listening to music can raise the brain's internal endorphin levels (which generate pleasure) even faster and more effectively than taking drugs can.

True pleasure is much more than a mere drug-induced sensation—it is a natural response to a pleasurable real-world experience in the present—but most drug users aren't aware of this distinction. Certainly if the drug user could compare the two forms of pleasure side by side, he would undoubtedly choose experiential pleasure over drug-induced sensation. It really and truly is that much better.

An excellent example of this can be seen in the nature of the sex act itself. Just about everyone will agree that real-world sex with a live partner is much more pleasurable than simple self-stimulation or the mere visualization of sex while one is alone. But it isn't just sex which is better as a real-world experience: every type of pleasure is better when it is experienced as a real-world activity. Indeed, if you were to take the drug abuser's notion of pleasure to its most extreme end point, it would be a totally disembodied (but viable) brain soaking in a concentrated solution of mind-altering chemicals!

The drug abuser prides himself on being a hedonist, a lover of pleasure. But as we have just seen, the road to true pleasure involves much more than the mere taking of a few pills. From this point of view, experiencing true pleasure is like anything else in this world: you've got to work hard for the things which are really worth having in life. There's no "free lunch" anywhere in the cosmos, but especially in the drug-using sector. Consequently, if the self-proclaimed hedonists of the drug-using

world are ever going to experience genuine pleasure, they are going to
have to rise to the occasion and give up their habit once and for all.

All in all, then, there are three general principles which one must
follow in order to experience true pleasure in life: (1) One must open
oneself up to the possibility of experiencing true pleasure in the present
by eliminating as many of one's historically based hangups as possible.
(2) One must not seek out shortcuts to pleasure; one must always choose a
real-world behavior over a biochemical shortcut to pleasure. (3) One
must keep one's mind as clear as possible of all intoxicants and pollutants
so that one can experience a pleasurable event as fully as possible.

In reference to Principle 3, it must always be remembered that pleasure is not contained in a pill; it is something the brain does for itself.
Moreover, it is something the brain does perfectly well on its own. It
therefore follows that if we try to improve on an already perfect neurological system, it is bound to malfunction, thereby producing less than
optimal amounts of pleasure in the long run.

It must never be forgotten that the human brain is the single most
complicated thing in the entire known universe. In fact, it's unbelievably
intricate web of neurological tissue is so complex that it makes the space
shuttle seem like a mere toy in comparison! With this in mind, who are
we to second-guess the Great Creator of the brain through the deliberate
ingestion of mind-altering chemicals? Do we think that we can improve
on His great design by adding poisonous foreign substances to our own
brain chemistry? Surely, God knew what He was doing when He designed
the brain the way He did, so shouldn't we trust that design and leave well
enough alone?[43]

The sports car enthusiast doesn't add orange juice, milk, or sugar to
his gas tank looking for better performance; he simply takes the manufacturer at his word and uses only the highest quality gasoline that he can
find, out of fear of ruining his machine. In the same way, we should
never deliberately ingest mind-altering chemicals looking for better
mental performance. We should instead take the Manufacturer at His
Word and let the brain function on its own. After all, who's to say exactly
what permanent effect a given drug will have on the unfathomably
complex bio-circuitry of the brain? It may be okay to gamble on a

---

43. In obvious cases of organic and/or behavioral pathology, it may be necessary to externally alter a
patient's brain chemistry in order to effect a positive result. However, the goal should always be to restore
normal functioning through a manipulation of naturally occurring substances (orthomolecular therapy),
not to create a new state of mind with xenobiotic (foreign) chemicals.

football game or at a casino, but it doesn't make any sense at all to gamble on the future integrity of our most precious possession in the entire world: our own personality. The stakes are simply much too high to justify the risk.

6.4 Other Hazards Associated With Drug Abuse

As we saw in the last chapter, there are a great many health problems which can result from chronic drug abuse. The list is seemingly endless. For instance, it is now a scientific fact that chronic drug use weakens the immune system, and that this weakening can render us much more susceptible to such diseases as AIDS, cancer, and the common cold; it can also cause our bodies to age faster than they otherwise would through the excessive production of chemical entities known as free radicals.

Another very real danger from I.V. drug use is the contracting of the AIDS virus through the sharing of needles. Addicts who share needles also run a higher risk of contracting hepatitis and other local and systemic infections.

However, perhaps the most serious health danger from chronic drug use involves sudden death by accident. Virtually all psychoactive drugs reduce our level of awareness and our ability to respond to a sudden stimulus, so when a person who is on drugs gets behind the wheel, an accident is MUCH more likely to happen. Some 55,000 people die every year in this country from auto accidents, and nearly half of them involve alcohol and/or drug use as the primary causative factor.

Indeed, who's to say how many major tragedies involving great losses of life are the result of drugs or alcohol? Certainly there is nothing at the present to prevent airline pilots, shipping captains, and railroad engineers from taking drugs while on the job. In fact, in a January 1987 railroad accident involving an Amtrak train which killed some sixteen people and injured over a hundred more, both engineers were shown to have had significant traces of marijuana in their blood.

There's no doubt about it. We live in an extremely precise, fast-paced world where a few inches can mean the difference between life and death. Therefore, it is imperative that we stay as straight as possible, especially when operating a motor vehicle or other heavy machinery, because we simply can't afford to let even the briefest drug-induced lapse in consciousness happen to us.

Another hazard of drug use involves the law. Whenever we do something illegal, there is always the distinct possibility that we will get caught, and getting caught using drugs or even "just" drunk driving can ruin our lives—sometimes forever. To be sure, no intoxicating substance is worth the risk of a permanently damaged life.

A more subtle hazard associated with drug use involves the lack of character growth which often accompanies the chronic use of drugs. Many psychoactive drugs have the frightening ability to act as a "developmental anchor" by tying us to whatever stage of development we happen to be in at the time. Thus, if we started taking drugs at the age of twenty-one and have gotten high on a daily basis through age thirty-one, it is quite possible that several of our most important personality characteristics will have remained effectively "frozen" at the age twenty-one level, precisely because of this growth-inhibiting effect of chronic drug use.

However, this drug-induced retarding of development isn't just a chemical effect of certain drugs; it also results from the fact that many people use drugs as a psychological defense in order to keep from facing unpleasant things about themselves. However, in order for a person to continue growing at a respectable pace, these unwanted parts of the personality must be owned up to and properly dealt with. Otherwise, by continuing to avoid them through the use of powerful psychoactive substances, the drug abuser inadvertently sentences himself to a lifetime of psychological stagnation.

This type of drug-induced retarding of development can have extremely tragic effects on a person's life in the world. For one thing, it can prevent a person from ever attaining his or her true potential in life. This alone is a tragedy worth mourning over. There's no doubt about it: when a chronic drug abuser reaches his fiftieth birthday and realizes that he is still in the same old humiliating job, he is bound to become seriously depressed, especially if he had the ability to do much more with his life but was prevented from doing so because of drugs. A great many career and personal opportunities present themselves to us over a lifetime, but if our lives are messed up with drugs, we could very well end up passing over a few golden opportunities that we will later regret.

Another subtle hazard which often results from chronic drug use is the setting of bad behavioral examples for others. Whether they intend to or not, adults who abuse drugs automatically set bad behavioral examples for both adults and children, and this can end up having the bad effect of encouraging other people to abuse drugs as well. Indeed, children are especially vulnerable to this type of behavioral influence. So, if you are a parent who has decided to continue using drugs, you should know that you run the risk of giving your children the unspoken message that drugs are okay to use, and that this sets them up for a possible lifetime of drug use themselves. Parents need to practice what they preach, because kids aren't dumb. They learn by imitating, so if their parents openly use drugs, the kids are more likely to do the same at some point in their development.[44]

Another very real danger which often results from chronic drug use is the antagonizing of important family members. Whether we are a teen-ager or a full-grown adult, our loved ones definitely do not want to see us get all caught up with drug abuse. So, if we insist on repeatedly getting high in spite of their pleas to the contrary, we run the serious risk of antagonizing them for life, and it simply isn't worth it to do so. Life is much too short and precious to waste it by arguing needlessly about drugs and alcohol. After all, our loved ones are all we really have in life; if we lose them, we lose just about everything. So, for the sake of maintaining good relationships with our loved ones, it makes sense to stay away from drugs as much as possible.

These are only a few of the many dangers which are inherent in drug use. And seeing how life itself is full of enough dangers and challenges, it doesn't make any sense at all to make things worse by acquiring the drug habit or by continuing to use drugs. You need to be good to yourself, because you really are your own best friend. And the best way to start being good to yourself is by swearing in your innermost heart of hearts that you will NEVER EVER use drugs, or if you are already using, that you will do your very best to kick the drug habit as soon as possible.

---

44. Sometimes, a parent who has totally ruined her life with drugs will inadvertently end up sending the opposite message to her kids, namely, that drugs are bad and so should never be used for any reason.

Chapter 7

THE BENEFITS OF DRUG USE

In order to be fair we will now consider the potential benefits of drug use.

The first of these benefits concerns the possible enhancement of a person's daily conscious experience. When drugs are used "properly"[45] (if that is even possible), one's conscious awareness of certain things can sometimes appear to be dramatically enhanced. This can lead to a feeling of greater intelligence and overall competence. However, most of the time this apparently heightened state of awareness turns out to be merely a drug-induced illusion. Certainly, the vast majority of insights that we appear to gain while on a given drug tend to disappear entirely when the drug effect wears off. For example, prior to my bad experience with LSD I had a number of apparent cosmic revelations while on the drug, but much to my dismay they all disappeared into thin air as soon as I "came down" from the high.

Moreover, there is no guarantee that a given drug will end up enhancing our overall awareness. Indeed, if anything, our awareness can just as easily become stifled and constricted through the use of drugs. Certainly the long-term use of just about any mind-altering chemical will end up having a deleterious effect on the mind. Consequently, it is foolish indeed to begin using drugs looking solely for consciousness expansion; there are simply a variety of safer and more efficient ways of doing so.

However, even if we assume for the sake of argument that certain drugs will enhance our conscious awareness, it doesn't logically follow that we should start a drug-using career. After all, many unpleasant experiences—such as being a prisoner of war for a year—also have the effect of raising our level of awareness, but no one in their right mind goes out of their way to have such an experience. Similarly, there is no

_____

45. By the proper use of a given drug I mean its limited use for the sole purpose of gaining a higher degree of consciousness from it. Several psychiatrists have used LSD for this very purpose over the years, with mixed results.

guarantee that a given drug will expand our awareness in a pleasant way, so it really isn't worth the risk to try it. There are simply a good many other, safer ways of expanding our consciousness.

It may be possible to kill a fly by blowing up a house, but no one does that because of the tremendous amount of destructive overkill that inevitably results. Similarly, it may be possible to raise one's conscious awareness by using psychoactive drugs, but in most cases it is senseless to do so because of the great amount of overkill that is inevitably produced, either in the present or in the future.

As far as my own case is concerned, I did in fact derive a great deal of intellectual benefit by going through my ordeal. It was like actually going to hell for several years and then coming back to tell the story. I learned a tremendous amount about the true meaning of life by going through my profound first-hand suffering. However, I would never want to go through such a horrendous experience again. Surviving a given tragedy may be able to grant a certain amount of growth and understanding to an individual, but no one in their right mind goes out of their way looking for a tragedy to jump into! By the same token, only a person who is bent on self-destruction will begin using drugs looking for growth and development, since in virtually all such cases it is a tragedy waiting to happen.

Another potential benefit of drug use involves the paradoxical breaking down of certain developmental barriers in psychologically stagnant individuals. As we grow into adulthood, our personality in life gradually solidifies, thereby effectively locking us into whatever cognitive set we happen to have attained for ourselves. If this cognitive set is pathological, it will tend to remain pathological for life unless something especially traumatic comes along to weaken the "psychological cement" of the mind, so that the contents of the personality can then be rearranged in a healthier fashion. Discreet drug use can often function as this type of "psychological solvent," which will permit the dissolution and subsequent rearrangement of the mind's solidified mental set.

On the downside, though, there is a serious risk of insanity whenever this type of drug-induced dismantling of personality is attempted. The reason for this is not far to seek: Any loosening of the mind's psychological cement will automatically cause the basic structure of the mind to be progressively dissolved, thereby causing a profound mental disorganization and loss of repression which in turn can unleash a serious bout of insanity in people. If this insanity is tolerated, it is possible to rearrange the freed-up components of the personality in a healthier overall matrix. However, it is equally possible that such a rearrangement will fail, thereby rendering the individual insane forever. Clearly, the risk/benefit ratio for this type of personality "therapy" is far too top-heavy to ever justify its use by the prudent individual.

Sometimes, the evil of getting hooked on drugs can paradoxically lead to a greater overall good in the long run by bringing what is sick on the inside out into the open, where it can be recognized for what it is and dealt with appropriately. Certainly if this inner sickness remains hidden, it will serve to make a person miserable for the duration of his life. Persistent drug abuse can be a symptom of this deeper illness, and insofar as it brings this illness out into the open where it can be recognized for what it is and subsequently cured, it ultimately does the individual a service instead of a disservice.

At the same time, though, if a person's abuse is too extreme, the drugs will end up destroying his life before he has a chance to get rid of his inner illness. Clearly, there is an extremely fine line which separates the character-redeeming potential goodness of drug abuse from its closely associated character-destroying badness. With this in mind, it can only be hoped that the drug abuser will be able to grow beyond his addiction by getting rid of his inner illness before his addiction gets rid of him.

7.1 Beneficial Side Effects of Drug Withdrawal

There are several positive side effects which can result from a successful withdrawal from drug addiction, above and beyond the actual kicking of the drug habit.

One of these potential benefits involves a radical changeover to a much healthier way of life. In order to be able to get through a bout of withdrawal most addicts need to start taking better care of themselves. This is most often done by starting an exercise program, eating a better diet, taking vitamins, and the like. These health-preserving behaviors can in turn help to improve and extend the ex-addict's life by making him less susceptible to such degenerative diseases as cancer, stroke, and heart disease.

Withdrawing from drugs can also have the beneficial effect of temporarily weakening the addict's psychological defense system, thereby enabling him to face and to feel repressions which would otherwise be buried deep in his unconscious. This emotional purging can have the effect of leading to a much less neurotic mindset, which can in turn help one to live a much healthier and happier life in the present. It can also serve to greatly lessen the addict's need for painkilling drugs for the following simple reason: the more an individual feels a formerly repressed feeling from his past, the less negative power it has over his life, which in turn means the less he has to resort to painkilling drugs to get rid of it.

Another potential benefit to a successful withdrawal program involves the inner spiritual transformation which often simultaneously takes place when a drug is withdrawn. Indeed, the deep-seated attitude conversion which absolutely must occur before the addict can successfully give up his habit closely parallels the type of attitude conversion seen in Christian conversion. Intense drug use can facilitate this saving attitude conversion by literally forcing the issue by showing the addict how desperately he needs to change. Then, when he finally changes his attitude enough to enable him to kick his drug habit, his newfound attitude will subsequently help to propel him through an incredibly beneficial series of spiritual transformations.[46]

In Christian circles this attitude conversion is called being "born again," and for good reason: one really is born again in the sense of having a whole new outlook and opportunity in life.

Interestingly enough, if a person can tap into this religious aspect of withdrawal, he can greatly improve his chances of a successful recovery. Alcoholics Anonymous, the immensely successful organization whose major purpose is to promote sobriety, has capitalized heavily on the religious nature of withdrawal and abstinence by utilizing a number of religious principles in its treatment program, including a belief in a "higher power." In so doing it has been remarkably successful in keeping alcoholics away from the bottle.

The spiritual transformation we are referring to here typically involves a good deal more than a "simple" attitude conversion. On the contrary, a radically transformed attitude can act as the initial stimulus for setting a whole new series of constructive behavioral events into motion. These novel behavior patterns in turn will usually begin to create a completely new daily experience for the ex-addict. Whereas before his conversion he

---

46. This process of spiritual transformation doesn't happen to everyone who undergoes withdrawal. It only happens to those who sincerely want to change and who are open to such radical personality-changing events. Many people go through withdrawal everyday because they have to, not because they want to; such reluctantly withdrawing individuals are thus not likely to experience a spiritual transformation when the drugs are out of their system. These are the people who are most likely to relapse soon after withdrawal is over.

may have been miserable, anxious, depressed, and unproductive in his day-to-day life, with his new behavior patterns he may suddenly find himself feeling happier, mellower, and more productive than he has felt in years.

Sometimes the inner spiritual transformation which often parallels withdrawal can end up leading the ex-addict to a happy and fulfilled religious life. Indeed, the feeling of having survived a profound spiritual test often has the effect of putting the ex-addict a good deal closer to his Maker. Such a religious affiliation should be strongly encouraged in the ex-addict, if not for its own sake, then because of the fact that it makes a subsequent relapse *much* less likely.

Chapter 8

KICKING THE DRUG HABIT
ONCE AND FOR ALL

It has repeatedly been said that human beings can do anything they set their minds to. Such an optimistic statement is for the most part completely true. We really can do whatever we set our minds to do. All it takes is the right attitude, sufficient practical knowledge and, of course, enough willpower.

Such is the case with drug addiction. Anyone can kick the drug habit; millions of people have successfully done so over the years, and you can too if you have the right attitude and enough willpower.

However, more is needed than just willpower and the right attitude. You need to know how to kick the drug habit; otherwise, your reformed attitude will just get overwhelmed by the process of withdrawal and you will probably go back to using drugs on a chronic scale. The fact of the matter is that it is possible to withdraw from any size drug habit with a bare minimum of pain and discomfort; you just need to know how. You need to have the right game plan in order to win.

No one told me how to kick the drug habit. I had to figure out what to do as I went along, and after a good deal of improvising and experimentation, I came up with a surefire way of getting off of drugs once and for all. It worked for me and it will work for you. All you've got to do is give it an honest shot (no pun intended!).

The protocol which follows is the tried-and-true product of an abuser's own first-hand battle with drugs. It isn't the sterile recommendation of a cold, disconnected clinician who has never even seen a joint; it is first-hand advice from someone who has been there. And to be sure, I'd rather listen to someone who has been where I want to go than to someone who's never been there. There are some things in life that you

107

simply can't learn from books, and kicking the drug habit is one of them.[47]

8.1 Warning

Before I begin with the "Increasing-Interval" and "Fixed-Reduction Rate" methods for kicking the drug habit, I must warn you that if you are addicted to any of the "hard" physically addicting drugs such as heroin, alcohol, or barbiturates, it would be best for you to seek out the best medical care available before you set out to undergo withdrawal. Even when they're properly managed, many courses of withdrawal from deep addictions can cause profound malaise and even death, so in these instances it is best to have a professional medical team on hand. At the same time, though, most of the following principles can still be utilized to make withdrawal and the post-withdrawal period as smooth and painless as possible.

8.2 A Step-By-Step Guide to Virtually Painless Drug Withdrawal

8.2.1 Step I: Attitude Conversion

Without a doubt the single most important factor in a successful course of withdrawal is the individual's own attitude. If the abuser doesn't realize that he has a problem and if he doesn't really want to get better with every fiber of his being, then it is pointless to go any further. Getting off of drugs isn't an externally administered cure like the removal of a ruptured appendix. It is an internally administered cure which requires first and foremost the person's own conviction and cooperation. Otherwise, the process of withdrawal is doomed to an early failure.

In many hard-core cases this commitment to change isn't hard to come by, because the addict's life has usually become so totally aversive that he or she desperately wants to kick the drug habit as soon as possible. It isn't easy being totally enslaved to a chemical god, so when the opportunity for breaking free finally presents itself, it is often warmly embraced. After all, the addict's whole life has been ruined by drugs, so unless his head is in the sand, he should be well aware of the fact that he has a problem.

---

47. Of course, it is possible for a physician to learn how to manage a severely addicted patient from books, but that is about the extent of it. The actual process of staying off of drugs requires a good deal of first-hand knowledge in order to be truly effective.

At the same time, though, there are many other users who don't yet realize that they are in trouble. These are the individuals who haven't yet suffered their way into an inner desire for change. Indeed, because they are usually convinced that they don't have a problem, they may actually resent any type of suggestion to the contrary. Such individuals are next to impossible to treat successfully, because as long as they don't think that they have a problem, they will refuse to cooperate with any type of withdrawal program.

Sometimes a confrontational approach may help to convince the user of his dire condition and need to change. If the user's spouse, friends, priest, and family all work together to confront him with the urgency of his problem and his desperate need to change, he just might see the light and consent to professional treatment.

The key, however, to getting through to such an individual is to only approach him when he is relatively straight, because this is perhaps the only time when he may be lucid enough to fully understand you. Unfortunately, though, most hard-core addicts are stoned all the time, so finding a lucid moment can tend to be rather difficult. Therefore, the best time to approach such a perpetually drugged individual is just after he awakens, since his system is as clean as it ever gets at that point.

As any family member of a severe "druggie" will agree, motivating the unrepentant addict to seek professional help is usually next to impossible. Committed addicts don't want to withdraw from their chosen poison, they don't want to enter the sterile environment of a hospital detoxification ward, and, perhaps most importantly, they don't want to face their true inner problems. In short, they don't want to face the fact that have failed again at the game of life, because it can easily turn out to be the final blow to their already fragile ego structure. On the other hand, it is common knowledge in the ex-addict population that a serious drug abuser must first "hit bottom" before he can truly effect change in his life. Consequently, if the committed addict can be talked into entering a professional treatment program, the shock of being a "drug patient" can often provide the necessary impetus for hitting bottom in this manner, thus allowing real progress to finally occur.

The best way of persuading an addict to seek help is to get him to conclude on his own that it is the best thing for him to do. One way to do this is to refer to the recent drug-induced fatality of one of his friends or family members and then to ask him the following question: If the victim's family could go back in time to a month before his drug-induced death, what could they have possibly done to prevent it? If he says that they should have put him in a professional detoxification ward, tell him that they already tried to do that and were unsuccessful. *The object is to get him to see that HE is currently in the same situation that the victim was in before he died.* If he denies that he is that bad off, tell him that that was exactly how the victim felt before he inadvertently died. Tell him that drugs are biochemically deadly by their very nature, so they will end up killing him too sooner or later. Tell him that the reason you are so concerned is that you love him and want the best for him.

If you are persuasive enough, you may eventually succeed in motivating him to seek out treatment. Unfortunately, though, such a persuasive success is rare indeed. More often than not, the addict's life must get intolerably unpleasant on its own before he will finally agree to change for the better.[48]

In those instances where the addiction has gotten out of hand and the user is totally uncooperative, an involuntary commission to a drug detoxification ward may be the best—if not the only—available alternative. Tens of thousands of drug-induced fatalities occur every year because the victims weren't rescued in time by their loved ones. However, committing an addict to a hospital against his will is much easier said than done. Because of the laws surrounding involuntary commission, you have to go through a lot of red tape before anything constructive ever gets accomplished. Moreover, just the casual mentioning of an involuntary commission in the presence of an abuser can cause him to become violent; so extreme caution is always appropriate when considering this option.

Unfortunately, even an involuntary commission to the best treatment program money can buy isn't always successful. Sometimes the underlying psychological problems which motivate the addiction aren't properly dealt with, so once the addict is released, he can't help but go straight back to his former habit. More typically, though, the act of being committed against his will causes the addict to remain uncooperative and unrepentant throughout his entire hospital stay. This virtually guarantees a relapse when the addict is finally released.

In such extreme instances, it appears as though the only thing which will ever rescue a hardened unrepentant addict from a lifetime of drug

---

48. Unfortunately, allowing an addict's life to get intolerably unpleasant on its own involves the very real risk of serious health damage or even death. The hope of course is that the addict will get miserable enough to change without actually dying or getting irreparably sick in the process.

addiction is hitting bottom through a truly catastrophic experience with drugs. There's no doubt about it: if the addict's drug use becomes aversive enough, he will naturally want to give up his habit, no matter how deeply ingrained it is. Otherwise, he will most likely continue taking drugs indefinitely. Unfortunately, though, waiting for this aversive threshold to be reached inevitably involves the risk of permanent health damage and even outright death!

8.2.2 Step II: The Process of Detoxification

Assuming that we have the abuser's pledge to do everything in his power to get off of drugs, we can now go on to Step II of the withdrawal process. In Step II we begin the actual shrinking of the abuser's daily dose of drugs.

There are only two major methods of drug detoxification: (1) an immediate cessation of all drug use ("cold turkey") and (2) a gradual reduction in drug dosage over a period of days or weeks.

The type of detoxification method which is most appropriate for you is dependent on two factors: (1) the drug you are hooked on and (2) the depth of your addiction. In general, the more addicting the drug and/or the deeper the habit, the more you need to follow a gradual process of dose reduction, while the less addicting the drug and/or the lighter the habit, the more you need to follow a cold turkey type of withdrawal program.

For example, if the drug is marijuana, nicotine, or caffeine, going cold turkey often works best, because the abstinence syndromes for these relatively mild drugs are usually a good deal less serious than those of the harder, more physically addicting drugs. In these cases, the distressing withdrawal symptoms which rapidly follow the cessation of drug use can usually be greatly reduced or eliminated with the proper treatment techniques (which are discussed later in this chapter). On the other hand, if the drug is a narcotic, a barbiturate, or ethyl alcohol, then going cold turkey can be extremely hazardous or even fatal. In these instances, a gradual reduction in dosage is usually most appropriate.[49]

As far as stimulant drugs such as cocaine and amphetamines are concerned, it has been said that they are not physically addicting in the classic morphine-like sense. But as we have already seen, these drugs are ferociously addicting in their own devilish way. Following the abrupt

---

49. The phrase "cold turkey" originated as a description of the cold "gooseflesh" skin which is often seen in the addict who is withdrawing from narcotics.

cessation of long-term use, severe withdrawal symptoms generally present themselves. Consequently, a gradual reduction in dosage is usually most appropriate for these drugs as well.

Many drug users are under the false assumption that just because a given psychoactive drug isn't physically addicting, it won't produce a disagreeable abstinence syndrome. Such an assumption couldn't be farther from the truth, for while a given psychoactive drug may not be physically addicting, it can still be addicting as far as one's conscious state of mind is concerned. This is because chronic use of these "non-addicting" psychoactive drugs usually causes a fundamental reorganization of the individual's mental state, which then disappears suddenly during withdrawal. It is this disappearance of a long-standing, drug-induced mental state which causes the withdrawal syndromes associated with these drugs.

In short, any drug which produces a noticeable change in a person's state of mind will produce a type of withdrawal syndrome when it is abruptly discontinued following prolonged use. Major tranquilizers such as Thorazine and antidepressants such as Sinequan are a good example: although they are not physically addicting in the classic sense, they still cause their own unique abstinence syndrome when they are withdrawn. For any such "non-addicting" drug, either the Increasing-Interval method or the Fixed-Reduction Rate method can be used to greatly reduce or even eliminate the discomfort of withdrawal.

A good rule of thumb to follow in trying to decide which method of drug detoxification is best (especially with the harder, physically addicting drugs) is *the deeper the habit, the more intense the withdrawal syndrome.* Thus if your habit is extensive, you can bet that your withdrawal syndrome will be equally extensive, so going cold turkey is probably out of the question (unless you are the self-professed heroic type!). However, if your habit is minimal, say only a few days old, you might be able to go cold turkey with very little problem.

The beauty of the Increasing-Interval method of drug detoxification is that it can easily be adapted to virtually any type of drug and any extent of addiction with very little alteration. The basic principles are the same whether the drug is heroin or Valium. Moreover, if you are trying to go cold turkey off of a relatively mild drug such as marijuana and find the going a bit too rough, you can instantly utilize the Increasing-Interval method to help you along without batting an eye.

Indeed, this is why I am convinced that the Increasing-Interval method for drug withdrawal is the best detoxification method of all: because its universal applicability to essentially all drugs and all degrees of addiction shows that it is the most appropriate method for the body's own physiological needs. For while the drug may be different in different addictions, the nature of the addictive process itself is similar among the different drugs. The Increasing-Interval method for drug detoxification naturally adapts itself to this physiological process of addiction and so is the most natural way to gradually eliminate chemical addictions in the body.

8.2.3 The Increasing-Interval and Fixed-Reduction Rate Detoxification Methods for Relatively Mild Drugs

As I mentioned earlier, it is often possible to go cold turkey off of such relatively mild drugs as marijuana, nicotine, or caffeine because their abstinence syndromes are so slight when compared with those of heroin or secobarbital.[50] Whatever discomfort which does arise can usually be promptly eliminated by using the anxiety-modulating techniques discussed later in this chapter. Nevertheless, if you have used these techniques and still find going cold turkey a bit too unpleasant, you can easily invoke a mild form of the Increasing-Interval method to reduce your discomfort to essentially zero.

Here's what to do. Once you decide to begin the withdrawal process, go cold turkey for as long as you can possibly stand it without losing your mind or getting inordinately uncomfortable. Then, at the peak of your discomfort, consume just enough of the drug you're hooked on to reduce your discomfort to tolerable levels; this usually amounts to only a puff or two of a cigarette or joint or a fraction of a pill. Repeat the procedure by again going cold turkey for as long as possible. If you do this faithfully, you will usually find that the interval between your drug "pit stops" will get progressively longer and longer. Pretty soon, it will be hours and then days between pit stops, and then before you know it, you will finally be totally free of your drug habit. But remember, you're only supposed to be taking enough drug to quell your withdrawal symptoms, not enough to get high.

For those of you who prefer a more structured method of detoxification, simply establish a daily regimen where you gradually reduce your daily dosage by a certain fixed amount every day. This is the Fixed-Reduction

---

50. Interestingly enough, many former heroin addicts have reported that it was easier to give up heroin than cigarettes!

Rate method for drug detoxification. For example, if you are trying to kick a pack-a-day cigarette habit, you might want to smoke two less cigarettes on each successive day until you eventually reach the magic figure of zero. For example, the first day you might smoke eighteen cigarettes, the second day sixteen cigarettes, and so on until you reach no cigarettes at all on the tenth day.

A primary advantage of this Fixed-Reduction Rate method is that it is more structured and hence easier to follow for some people than the Increasing-Interval method. Its greatest advantage, though, is that it tends to minimize the temporary withdrawal discomforts which are seen in the Increasing-Interval method, since you aren't trying to go as long as you can without taking anything—you are simply taking a fixed dosage of drug on each successive day. Nevertheless, when your daily dosage drops far enough, you may find yourself strategically arranging your doses in an Increasing-Interval manner so as to get the most advantage from them.

A major disadvantage of the Fixed-Reduction Rate method is that it is usually a lengthier process than the Increasing-Interval method. It is also less tuned to the body's own unique physiological needs than is the Increasing-Interval method. In the latter method, you adjust the timing and quantity of each dose to fit your own bodily requirements, whereas in the former method you simply take a fixed dosage at the most convenient times during the day.

8.2.4 The Increasing-Interval and Fixed-Reduction Rate Detoxification Methods for the Harder, More Addicting Drugs

As I mentioned earlier, if the drug you're trying to kick is a powerful, physically addicting narcotic or other CNS depressant (like heroin, Percodan, phenobarbital, Valium, or alcohol), then going cold turkey is NOT the thing to do because it could prove to be life-threatening, especially in instances of pronounced alcohol or barbiturate addiction. Rather, the most prudent thing to do is to gradually reduce your daily intake until it eventually reaches zero. (The same process can be used to manage cocaine and amphetamine withdrawal with little or no modification.)

Again, you have two basic withdrawal methods to choose from: the Increasing-Interval method and the Fixed-Reduction Rate method. Choose whichever method you feel most comfortable with.

If you want to try the Increasing-Interval method, here's what to do. Say you are addicted to twenty Percodans a day. Try cutting back your daily dose by several pills for a few days in order to see how you do. How many pills you cut back on should be adjusted to your own bodily requirements, not for getting high, but for blocking any withdrawal symptoms. If you can get by on only twelve pills a day, then by all means do so, but if you can only go down to eighteen pills without experiencing undue discomfort, then you shouldn't try to cut back any further. As always, try to take a dose only when you feel you absolutely have to; in this way the pace of withdrawal can be tailored to your own unique bodily requirements. When you feel you can tolerate it, you should try to drop your daily dosage down to the next level where you feel moderately comfortable. Of course, due to the physiological differences in people, the actual pace of any given course of withdrawal will be different for different people.

During each reduction you should space the pills out so that their consumption is most effective. For example, if you find that you can go five hours without taking more than a pill or two, by all means do so; then, when the aversiveness starts to build again, you can quell it by taking your next dose of drug.

Often, a full dose won't even be necessary in order to quell most of your withdrawal symptoms. This is because the amount of drug that is needed to forestall withdrawal symptoms is usually far less than the amount needed to make you high. In these cases you should attempt to get by using the smallest possible dose of drug at each "pit stop." For example, if you're trying to get by on eight Percodans a day and following your morning dose of two pills you find yourself getting uncomfortable in the afternoon, you shouldn't just blindly take two more pills. Rather, take only a half a pill at first and see how you do. If that turns out to be insufficient, take a little more until you feel tolerably comfortable. Again, the idea is to go for as long a time as possible on as little drug as possible.

By using the various anxiety-reducing techniques discussed later in this chapter in concert with the Increasing-Interval method for detoxification, you can exert a great deal of control over how long you can go between pit stops, how much drug you need at each pit stop, and how you feel in general. Indeed, a mega-dose of buffered vitamin C powder or a brisk walk around the block can often take the place of a pill or two, thereby enabling you to last longer on a given dose of drug.

If after a few days you find that you can comfortably tolerate your current dosage level, the next thing to do is to cut your daily dose back again. Ideally you won't have to consciously implement this reduction, your body will do the reducing for you, i.e. if you closely follow your own bodily requirements, taking the smallest effective dose each time, you may very well find your cumulative daily dose to be gradually shrinking on its own. Sometimes, though, if we let our bodies alone decide how much to take we may find ourselves inadvertently upping the dosage; this occurs most often when we exceed the minimum dose necessary to forestall withdrawal symptoms. These are the times when we must literally force our bodies to accept an externally administered reduction in dosage.

In these instances it may be easier for you to resort to the Fixed-Reduction Rate method of drug withdrawal, so that you can predetermine the number of pills or drinks you will be taking on each successive day. But even if you do, you may still find yourself using the Increasing-Interval method to help you get by when your dosage gets particularly low, i.e. you may find yourself trying to get by on the lowest effective dose at each pit stop so as to be able to conserve the amount of drug remaining for the rest of the day. This type of conservation is especially effective if the drug you're trying to kick is a CNS depressant, because the more milligrams you are able to "stockpile" until bedtime, the better you will probably sleep the rest of the night.

Actually, most withdrawal regimens involve some combination of these two methods. For example, if you are trying to do 50 percent reductions on an original twenty-pill-a-day habit, your first dosage reduction will take you from twenty pills to ten pills, or one-half of your original dose, while your second reduction will take you from ten pills to five pills, or one-quarter of your original dose, and so on. This is a fixed rate of dosage reduction. But since each reduction will most likely cause some degree of discomfort, you will need to use the Increasing-Interval method of strategically placing your doses, along with the pain-limiting procedures outlined in the next section of this chapter, to be able to comfortably tolerate each drop in dosage.

Of course, different people will follow different time courses during withdrawal. Some will find that they can only tolerate cutting back by an eighth of their original dose each time instead of a quarter, while others will find that they will be able to cut their daily dose by half every day until they are totally clean in a few days. The key is to pay close attention to your body and to utilize the regimen which works best for you.

It is truly amazing how effective a relatively tiny dose of drug can be during withdrawal if your suffering is particularly acute. Indeed, the effectiveness of a given small dose in quelling withdrawal symptoms seems to be directly related to the amount of suffering you are able to tolerate: the longer you are able to go without a dose, and hence the more you are able to suffer, the less drug your body will require at each pit stop to feel near normal, at least for a time. The duration of this feeling of near normalcy following a mini-dose will gradually lengthen, especially if you are able to tolerate a great deal of suffering between doses.

It is almost as if you are able to "buy" each reduction in dosage with the degree and extent of suffering that you can tolerate, and in fact this is what actually happens on a biochemical level: as the drug slowly drains from the body's tissues, the body struggles to restore its own "homeostasis" or balance, and it is this biochemical struggling which produces the suffering. The more suffering, the more drug that is drained from the body; the more drug that is drained from the body, the less drug the body has to become acclimated to, hence the less drug the body needs to have its withdrawal pangs quelled.

Again, the best part of this Increasing-Interval method of drug detoxification is that you can tailor the pace of your withdrawal to suit your own needs and tastes. For example, if you are feeling particularly heroic, you can shorten the withdrawal process by using smaller doses and larger intervals; while this speeds things up, it of course also increases the amount of pain involved. On the other hand, if you want to minimize your suffering and time is no object, you can use larger doses and smaller interval times.

Happily, the actual process isn't nearly as hard as it sounds. Once you get the hang of it, it is easy to adjust the doses and intervals you use (and hence the pace of your withdrawal) to your own bodily needs.

As far as alcohol withdrawal is concerned, the same basic procedure can be followed. However, it is important to realize that withdrawal from a bona fide alcohol addiction is potentially much more serious than withdrawal from opiates or tranquilizers. Death can even result if the withdrawal isn't properly managed, so going cold turkey is most definitely NOT the thing to do.

Therefore, if at all possible the alcoholic should seek professional inpatient treatment before undergoing withdrawal (as should all individuals with deep-seated addictions). Fortunately, because of the widespread nature of alcoholism among the middle and upper classes, the traditional medical establishment has come up with some very effective procedures for managing alcohol withdrawal. Sadly, though, many of these programs concentrate only on the physical side of withdrawal and thus fail to deal with the pervasive anxiety that drives most alcoholics to drink in the first place. This is why so many alcoholics relapse after professional treatment.

Later in this chapter several potent anxiety-reducing techniques will be discussed which can be used to quell withdrawal symptoms in recovering addicts. These techniques are just as effective for the withdrawing alcoholic as they are for other substance abusers. Indeed, they are so effective that they should be a part of any treatment program, whether the alcoholic is being professionally supervised or not.

Because of the similarity of alcoholism to other "downer" addictions, the Increasing-Interval method of drug withdrawal should work fine if you are an alcoholic with a moderate to moderately severe habit. You should just take extreme care and go very slowly with the withdrawal process, using small alcohol-free intervals and sufficient doses to quell your most severe symptoms. At all times you should be on the lookout for the infamous "DT's" (delirium tremens); should you inadvertently experience a seizure or a period of delirium in spite of proper interval treatment, you should definitely seek out professional medical care. INDEED, IF AT ALL POSSIBLE YOU SHOULD WITHDRAW AS AN INPATIENT IN A PROFESSIONAL CLINIC. THIS INCREASING-INTERVAL METHOD IS ONLY FOR THOSE WHO REFUSE TO SEEK OUT SUCH TREATMENT OR FOR THOSE WHOSE HABITS AREN'T SO EXTENSIVE.

After the initial withdrawal period is over, many ex-alcoholics find membership in A.A. (Alcoholics' Anonymous) to be particularly helpful in preventing relapse. Similar support groups, such as N.A. (Narcotics' Anonymous), also exist for other drug problems.

As far as cocaine withdrawal is concerned, it is best to seek professional medical treatment if the addiction is particularly severe or if there is a predisposition to mental illness. Nevertheless, the cocaine addict can still get through a severe withdrawal episode in one piece if he faithfully uses the Increasing-Interval method already discussed, along with the anxiety-reducing techniques which will be discussed shortly.

In cases of multiple addictions, you must be doubly careful about withdrawing in a safe manner, since in many cases the effects of withdrawing from two drugs are more than additive. In these instances a professional detoxification clinic is probably your best bet.

Nevertheless, if your multiple drug habit isn't too extensive, you can use the same Increasing-Interval method to gradually withdraw from both drugs, one at a time. For example, if you are hooked on large daily doses of both Valium and Percodan, you might initially cut your daily dose of Valium back first while keeping your dose of Percodan the same. Then, after you stabilize on this new Valium dose a few days later, your Percodan dose can then be cut back as well. Once you are stabilized on this regimen, you can go through the same process over and over again until you are totally clean of both drugs. Again, the extent of each dosage reduction and the length of your drug-free intervals should be tailored to your own bodily requirements.

If cigarette smoking is further complicating the withdrawal picture, it might be best to wait until the drug withdrawal program is almost completed before attempting to give up cigarettes as well. The reason, of course, is that the body only has a limited ability to vanquish its addictions; therefore, you don't want to overload the body's own healing mechanisms by attempting to give up too much at once.

You must also be extremely careful about operating dangerous machinery during the withdrawal process, especially if you are withdrawing on your own outside of a hospital. It might be a good idea not to drive until the worst is over, since your withdrawal pangs could easily end up distracting your attention from the road enough to cause a serious accident.

Finally, if at all possible, it might help to temporarily move to a clean and picturesque area during withdrawal to help make the process easier. The clean air could easily strengthen your intrinsic defenses, especially if you live in a highly polluted area, and the scenic beauty could make the whole process a good deal more pleasant for you.

8.3 Withdrawal During Pregnancy

As we have already seen, any sort of unnecessary drug use during pregnancy is an extremely hazardous affair, due to the utter susceptibility of the growing fetus. All sorts of drug-induced birth defects can result if a woman makes the monumental mistake of taking drugs while she is pregnant. Worse yet, the teratogenic (fetus-damaging) effects of many prescription drugs won't be fully known for a number of years, so it is impossible to tell with any degree of certainty whether a particular new drug will end up damaging the fetus or not.

Consequently, the only prudent thing to do is to not smoke or take any drugs at all during pregnancy without a doctor's explicit order; even then, it pays to have a second opinion, because doctors have been dead wrong about these things an embarrassing number of times in the past. (Just witness the thousands of tragedies which have surrounded the medical use of thalidomide and DES.)

Withdrawal during pregnancy is an equally hazardous affair, since the physical stress can end up either damaging the fetus or causing a miscarriage. Ideally, it is best to not have to withdraw at all during pregnancy, but if you nevertheless happen to get pregnant while addicted, it is best to get off the drug as soon as possible, since the more you take of it, the more the fetus itself will be addicted.[51] There is nothing in the world more pitiful and sad than a baby born addicted to drugs.

If you are pregnant you should never attempt to withdraw from drugs on your own. This is the most hazardous time of all to attempt withdrawal, so you will definitely need professional medical supervision. But don't wait: get it over with as soon as possible, because the life of another human being absolutely depends on it. (Indeed, while you may feel morally free to damage your own body with drug abuse, you are definitely not morally free to damage another person's body with drugs, even if that person happens to be inside of your own body.)

8.4 Life-Style Changes Which Aid in the Withdrawal Process

Drug addiction is a health-destroying state of being. Like all health-destroying activities, it feeds on itself. But once the vicious cycle of addiction is broken by your decision to change, it becomes imperative for you to replace your anti-health life-style with a much more healthful way of life as soon as possible. This type of life-style change will not only allow your body and mind to heal properly, it will also allow you to eliminate your craving for drugs once and for all.

In order to be able to stay off of drugs indefinitely, then, a state of optimal physical health needs to be achieved and maintained. First and foremost, this means that all ingested substances which are not essential for bodily functioning should be eliminated as soon as possible, especially the toxic ones. Of course, the reason for this is that all the drugs you've ingested over the years have literally poisoned your body and mind, so much so that your biochemistry has actually adapted itself to the poison.

---

51. Depending on the extent of the pregnancy, it may be better to wait until a safer trimester to undergo withdrawal. A physician should always be consulted in such instances for the most appropriate advice.

Consequently, if you are ever going to reach an optimal state of health, you are absolutely going to have to eliminate as many toxins from your life as possible, above and beyond the drugs you've been taking.

The very first toxin you must eliminate is nicotine if you smoke. There's no two ways about it: if you are to ever permanently kick the drug habit, you are going to HAVE to quit smoking.

There are several very good reasons for this. First and foremost, nicotine is itself an extremely powerful addictive drug (some addicts have found it easier to give up heroin than to give up cigarettes), so if you're going to give up your addiction to all addicting drugs, you're going to have to get rid of cigarettes by definition. In addition, cigarette smoke contains over 1000 known poisons; these poisons contribute to your lack of wellness by keeping your system in a toxic state of being. Nicotine alone is so toxic that one purified drop of it is more than enough to kill you outright! And since being toxic is one aspect of the bio-phenomenon of addiction, continuing to smoke makes it more likely (at least in a biological sense) that you will eventually go back to using drugs again.

It may sound hard to understand, but it really isn't. The phenomenon of addiction occurs when the body adapts itself to the repeated presence of a poison. In fact, it adapts itself so much that when the poison is suddenly not there anymore, withdrawal symptoms develop. So, as long as you continue to ingest addictive poisons into your body, the whole bio-phenomenon of addiction remains active, and as long as it remains active, the more likely you are to go back to using drugs again. This is a prime example of the "spreading" phenomenon which is seen so often in biological systems.

Substitute addictions do take place, however, such as when cigarette and coffee addictions replace heroin addiction. And although cigarettes and coffee may be preferable to heroin on one level, such a substitution of one addiction for another doesn't represent a true cure or an optimal state of wellness. It is only a temporary "stopgap" procedure for people who need a biochemical crutch in order to survive. Indeed, what happens if the substitute addiction suddenly becomes no longer sufficient? Other, more serious addictions can easily end up taking its place, because the inner process of addiction hasn't been properly dealt with. This is why the only way to permanently overcome the addictive process once and for all is to give up all substitute addictions at the same time.

Another way of saying this involves the principle of the incompatibility of opposites. In order to make drug addiction as unlikely as possible, we need to maximize its opposite—optimal wellness—within the body, since genuine wellness automatically excludes the process of addiction, just as being wet automatically excludes being simultaneously dry. The principal reason for this is that drug addiction usually feeds off an unhealthy body, in the same way that the cold virus usually infects those people whose defenses are compromised in some way. A healthy body, on the other hand, is intrinsically safeguarded to a certain extent from becoming addicted by its very nature. It contributes to an overall sense of well-being which in turn makes the lure of drug abuse much less attractive, since there is no aversive physical or mental condition from which to escape.[52]

This is why you cannot continue to smoke if you genuinely want to get over your drug addiction once and for all: because as long as you smoke your health will be greatly compromised, and it is this lack of optimal healthfulness which leads to the system-wide bad feeling which in turn motivates one to begin using drugs. In other words, since most people take drugs to stop feeling bad, or simply to feel better, and since cigarette smoking makes most people feel worse through a direct poisoning of the body, it logically follows that smoking cigarettes makes it more likely that drugs will be resorted to to help one feel better.

The final reason why you need to quit smoking concerns the almost ubiquitous allergy to cigarette smoke in our society. Approximately three-fourths of the population are allergic to cigarette smoke in one way or another, but due to the very nature of addiction the majority of these people are likely to be smokers. This is because people often become addicted to the very things that they are allergic to. This is true of foods, drugs, and, of course, cigarettes.

An allergy to cigarette smoke can cause all sorts of unpleasant symptoms in people, and it is precisely these symptoms which greatly increase the likelihood of drug addiction, since they seem to put one in a negative, addictive frame of mind. Undoubtedly, the worst symptoms of all are manifestations of a syndrome known as cerebral allergy. The brain can react in an allergic fashion just as any other organ can, and when it does,

---

52. Nevertheless, there are many people in good physical shape who try drugs out of curiosity instead of desperation and who subsequently become addicted. Len Bias, for example, was one of the greatest athletes in the entire country, but his curiosity about cocaine eventually got the best of him and he died as a result. On the whole, though, the better physical shape one is in, the less likely one is to be driven by a state of physiological aversiveness into using drugs.

all manner of aversive psychiatric symptomatology can result. Indeed, just about every psychiatric symptom in the book can result from cerebral allergy, from hallucinations and schizophrenia to chronic anxiety attacks and psychotic depression.

In fact, in one study conducted at a major psychiatric institution, the majority of schizophrenic patients were found to be severely allergic to cigarette smoke. Even more remarkable is the fact that most of their symptoms completely disappeared when the allergen was removed from their environment! And as if that weren't enough, the experimenters were able to reproduce the schizophrenic symptoms at will by selectively re-exposing the patients to cigarette smoke!

It is the very insidiousness of cerebral allergy which makes it so difficult to identify and treat. Most people who start to experience psychiatric difficulty don't usually make the connection (if such a connection in fact exists) to an offending environmental chemical. They usually attribute it to some unpleasant event in their lives or to some other mysterious unknown cause. In many (if not most) of these cases the true cause of their bad feeling is an offending chemical in their environment.

Even worse is the fact that in genuine cases of cerebral allergy most doctors are also unable to make the necessary connection to the true causative agent. They simply assume that the patient is mentally disturbed, so they inadvertently make him worse by prescribing powerful drugs to "control" his symptoms. One thing, however, is certain: as long as cigarettes and other allergens are causing cerebral allergies in people, these individuals are going to remain in a greatly compromised state of health, and it is this greatly compromised state of health which makes it much more likely that they will resort to drugs looking for relief.

For example, let's say that Bob has gone through a successful program of narcotic withdrawal by using either the Increasing-Interval or the Fixed-Reduction Rate method of detoxification discussed previously. Unfortunately, though, Bob has continued to smoke, and unbeknownst to him, he has continued to experience profound cerebral allergies because of the smoke. Consequently, everytime he lights up he gets nervous, anxious, morbid, and depressed; however, since he is a chain smoker, his symptoms are so constant that it is impossible for him to identify his smoking as being the cause of them.

Even worse is the fact that Bob's cigarette-induced psychiatric symptoms make it much more likely that he will end up resorting to other drugs looking for relief. However, if he were to give up smoking once and for all, his negative cerebral reactions would cease and he would have much less reason to take drugs again. The moral of this hypothetical story is clear: all possible allergens which may be contributing to a case of cerebral allergy need to be eliminated before an individual will be optimally protected from the temptation of using drugs for symptom relief.

However, cigarettes aren't the only culprit when it comes to stimulating cerebral allergies. Thousands upon thousands of other substances are also capable of causing this problem, ranging from natural substances, such as pollen and cat hair, to synthetic substances, such as gasoline and industrial pollution.

Indeed, most people fail to realize that the very buildings they are living and working in can be making them sick. You'd be surprised how many people die every year in response to the routine use of various pesticides, herbicides, and other common chemical poisons. The Environmental Protection Agency has made progress in combating this serious health hazard by recognizing what it calls "sick building syndrome," which is basically a poorly ventilated building containing toxic chemical odors. Ironically enough, one of the first buildings to get cited as being "sick" was the EPA's own building in Washington, DC!

The notion that severe psychiatric symptoms can be the result of brain allergies is actually good news for millions of people, because it means that there is finally hope for their eventual recovery. Being unaware of the true cause of their suffering, many victims of cerebral allergy have concluded that they were simply born with the tendency to be disturbed and so are powerless to do anything about it. Consequently, hearing that their recovery could involve something so pedestrian as the removal of a particular offending substance from their environment gives many cerebral allergy sufferers a new lease on life.

All in all, cerebral allergy is an extremely widespread problem which is contributing a great deal to the spread of drug abuse in our society. Fortunately, there are medical experts known as "clinical ecologists" who specialize in treating this very problem. So, if you suspect that you might be experiencing a type of cerebral allergy, it is certainly in your best interest to have a consultation with a clinical ecologist as soon as possible.[53]

53. For a listing of the various clinical ecologists around the country, write to: The American Academy of Environmental Medicine, P.O. Box 16106, Denver, Co 80216.

8.5 The Drug-Induced Spiraling Effect Leading Towards Total Mental Collapse

As we have just seen, when negative reactions to the environment continue unabated in a susceptible individual, the individual is much more likely to turn to drug abuse for relief. However, dealing with one chemical reaction by ingesting another poisonous chemical greatly complicates matters within the brain and makes it more likely that the individual's mental status will begin the precipitous spiral which leads towards a total psychological collapse.

This process of spiraling into psychopathology is an exceedingly ominous and frightful phenomenon. It appears as though it is a pre-established response of the human mind to a particular set of inner conditions. These conditions involve a critical interplay between the physical brain and the spiritual mind; thus, they take full advantage of the human psyche's tremendous complexity by bringing a complete and total hell upon the unsuspecting individual who unknowingly creates the proper conditions for this spiraling effect to take place.

These conditions begin on a physical level, when the brain begins reacting in an unpleasant way to a particular environmental chemical or to a painful event in one's life. This initiates a certain amount of suffering and anxiety in the spiritual mind. It is here that a critical choice presents itself to the individual, and depending on the choice he makes, he will either stay free of the downward spiral or go one step closer towards its evil clutches.

If he chooses to respond to his negative reaction by avoiding the offending chemical, by psychotherapy, or by engaging in any number of relatively safe symptom-reducing techniques, such as exercising, eating, sleeping, or taking an aspirin, he will in all likelihood remain free from the evil spiral. However, if he chooses to respond to his negative reaction by ingesting a more dangerous psychoactive chemical, such as heroin, LSD, or cocaine, he will at once become much closer to the evil spiral. For once he attempts to treat his negative reaction with a powerful psychoactive drug, his brain biochemistry will suddenly become a good deal more muddled and confused. This biochemical complication will eventually produce even more suffering in the spiritual mind, which in turn will tempt the individual to ingest still more drugs in the pursuit of relief. It is this vicious cycle of trying to reduce mental suffering with drugs which eventually becomes transformed into the mental spiral which eventually leads to total mental collapse (see Figure 2).

The following analogy may help you to further visualize this downward-spiraling effect. Imagine a knot that is tied in a nerve string in the brain as the result of a painful life experience. Now if the nerve string is supposed to be straight for proper mental functioning, it follows that the individual should do all he can to untie the knot. However, imagine that instead of straightening out the knot, the drug abuser ties another knot, and then still another with drugs looking for relief. If he continues to do this, eventually the entire nerve string will break down and mental collapse will occur.

Figure 2

**How the Drug-Induced Spiraling Effect Leads Towards
Total Mental Collapse**

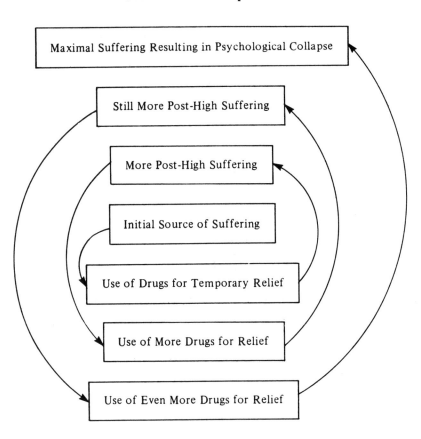

Once it is begun, the process of spiraling acts as if it were a whirlpool trying to suck you into its very center. Once you fall within its power, each step in the wrong direction brings you deeper and deeper into the spiral's evil clutches and thus makes it less and less likely that you will be able to escape its incredibly destructive effects. Unfortunately, the easy way out in such instances usually brings one closer to the center of the evil spiral, instead of further away.

Panicking of course only makes things worse. In such cases only a radical sort of intervention, such as a major trip to a foreign land or a new romantic relationship, coupled with a cessation of drug use and the appropriate orthomolecular treatment, might enable one to escape the lure of the downward spiral; otherwise, the power of this mental spiraling will get stronger and stronger with each passing moment, until eventually a total "nervous breakdown" will take place.

Clearly, the best way to avoid falling into the power of this evil spiral is to never treat any type of psychological discomfort with mind-altering chemicals in the first place. In this way the vicious cycle described above never gets started.[54] Other more healthful ways of dealing with psychological discomfort can instead be substituted, several of which will be discussed shortly.

This rule applies to tranquilizers such as Thorazine and Valium just as much as it applies to heroin and cocaine. Indeed, perhaps it is no accident that the majority of those people who are being treated with legitimately prescribed psychoactive drugs show some degree of serious psychopathology, i.e. perhaps the cure is worse than the disease—perhaps it is the drug treatment which is causing the abnormal behavior and not vice versa. Certainly by complicating a brain biochemistry that is already overwhelmed by a major stress reaction, toximolecular drug treatment has the power to transform stressed-out normal people into abnormal people by initiating the vicious drug-induced spiral which leads to total mental collapse.

In my own case this is clearly what happened. Instead of allowing me to react in a normal way to the various stresses in my life, my doctor prescribed a series of extremely toxic drugs for me to take. These drugs in turn overwhelmed my already overloaded brain biochemistry and

---

54. Actually, just about any self-destructive method of handling stress can lead to a similar type of downward spiral. This is why so many "straight" (i.e. non-drug using) people end up with nervous breakdowns.

sent me spiraling towards an unprecedented four-year bout with a drug-induced hell.

Tragically, millions of lives are still getting ruined every year by doctors who are continuing to prescribe these devilish poisons. What on earth makes these well-meaning physicians think that the xenobiotic (foreign) chemicals they are using in the name of "drug therapy" will be able to restore true normalcy to their patients? The fact of the matter is that if you give these potent drugs to "normal" people, they too will be made ill in a matter of hours (some in a matter of minutes). Consequently, what basis is there for thinking that so-called "abnormal people" will react any differently? After all, the majority of individuals with psychiatric symptoms are relatively normal people who are simply reacting to a major stressful event in their lives; their symptoms are thus usually only temporary. However, when they are treated with powerful psychiatric drugs in an unnatural effort to control symptoms, the drugs themselves can inadvertently cause them to REALLY get sick.

For millions of innocent people, then, the "cure" of tranquilizer use is worse than the disease. As such, it represents a fundamental violation of the physician's Hippocratic Oath to first do no harm. Indeed, how can doctors honestly expect sick people to be cured with these drugs when healthy people are made sick by them? After all, most psychiatric syndromes are not the result of bacterial infections which must be brought under control with powerful drugs that make normal people sick; they are instead simply the result of excessive psychobiological stress in people's lives.[55] Consequently, it follows that these relatively normal, stressed-out people need to be treated with substances that promote health in normal individuals, not take away from it. This is the theoretical basis underlying the relatively new discipline of orthomolecular psychiatry.

There's no doubt about it. Most of the stronger psychiatric drugs "work" because they act as "chemical straightjackets"; they are used because they keep otherwise troublesome patients under control with a minimum of work. But this isn't true therapy; it isn't restoring mental health to suffering people. It is the medically sanctioned destruction of character which has the approval of all but the most enlightened psychiatrists.

---

55. An exception to this observation is the mental dis-ease caused by a systemic infection with the yeast germ "Candida albicans." Even so, treating non-infected people with antifungal drugs isn't nearly as disastrous as treating mentally normal people with tranquilizers and antidepressants.

One way to prevent this downward spiral from happening to you is to avoid as much unnecessary psychological discomfort as possible in your life, especially in the sphere of chemical hypersensitivities. In this way you won't be motivated to turn to drugs looking for relief. This in turn entails daily relaxation therapy, as well as the elimination of everything in your immediate environment that you are sensitive to, both chemicals and foods. If you suspect that you have multiple allergies, it might be best to consult a clinical ecologist in order to find out exactly what you are allergic to so that you can then institute the appropriate treatment.

As far as food allergies are concerned, most people don't realize that they are often allergic to the very foods to which they are addicted. For example, if someone is addicted to Monterey Jack cheese, then the odds are very good that he or she will also be allergic to it. The reason for this paradoxical phenomenon involves the energy pickup many people initially get by eating foods which they are allergic to. When the pickup gives way to lethargy, they feel driven to eat the food again to regain the pickup. Eventually, this process grows into a bona fide addiction.

All in all, if you are to be truly successful in giving up your addiction to drugs, you must also do your best to eliminate the rest of your allergies and addictions as well, with the most important being cigarettes.

8.6 Step III: A Unified Support System for Dealing With Both the Pain of Withdrawal and the Anxiety of the Subsequent Drug-Free State

There are several extremely effective orthomolecular treatments which can be used both during and after withdrawal to greatly reduce or even eliminate the pain and anxiety of being drug-free.[56] A way of life more than anything else, these treatments can rapidly make you feel so much better about yourself—both physically and mentally—that your very craving for drugs should eventually disappear entirely.

The Proper Diet

The first step in our quest for optimal health involves eating the proper foods. Eating right is extremely important because an improper

---

56. The term "orthomolecular" literally means "straightening out" the molecules in the body. It involves using those substances which naturally occur in the body to treat illness and maximize health.

diet can make you sick, and as long as you are sick you are much more likely to resort to drugs looking for relief. On the other hand, following a good diet can make you feel terrific, and feeling good is perhaps the best way of all to innoculate yourself against the temptation of using mind-altering drugs.

The first thing we need to realize in our quest for the optimal diet plan is that it is usually the type and not the amount of food that is most important. Thus, as long as the right foods are eaten, it doesn't usually matter how much you actually eat (except of course in the case of red meat and other cholesterol-containing foods). This is a primary postulate of the famous Pritikin diet plan. It is a valid point because it is difficult to grossly overeat or to gain a lot of weight while eating the proper foods. The natural bulk and nutrition they contain make us feel full before we are actually able to overeat.

All whole fruits and vegetables are good to eat (except of course for those to which you are allergic). I emphasize the word "whole" because optimal nutrition only occurs when a person eats the whole fruit or vegetable: isolating a particular part of the food disrupts its critical nutrient balance and thus places an inordinate amount of stress on the body's digestive process, which naturally "expects" the proper balance of nutrients in the food that is eaten. So, if you are going to eat a baked potato, eat the skin too!

Whole-grain foods are also excellent. Stay away from overly processed, enriched grains, because their most nutritious parts have been processed away, leaving behind only the bare skeleton of grain. These culinary remnants pose a great deal of stress for the body when they are consumed, since such "foods" force the body to operate on fuels which have been stripped of most of their nutritive value. It's sort of like using extremely low-grade gasoline for a high-performance sports car—overall performance in both cases is bound to be severely compromised. So, instead of eating white enriched bread, try to eat whole-grain bread; instead of eating white rice, try to eat whole-grain brown rice, etc.

You can also eat meat but, of course, not in excessive quantity. A quarter-pound or so per day is okay, but even then you should try to "steer" away from red meat in favor of turkey and chicken. If you can find it, try to buy only "organically grown" meat, because it doesn't usually contain the DES, antibiotics, or other toxins that commercial meat is often contaminated with. Fish, of course, is great, assuming that it hasn't been contaminated with lead, mercury, or other toxins. A good rule of thumb to follow in determining the safety of a given fish is *the further out in the ocean that the fish is caught, the safer it generally is,* since man-made pollution tends to accumulate close to shore. Tragically, though, toxic waste has become so ubiquitous in our relatively tiny world that almost nothing is completely safe to eat anymore.[57]

On the positive side, fish body oils (Max EPA) have been shown to prevent blood clots and to significantly lower both cholesterol and triglyceride levels in the blood, thereby lowering heart attack rates. This is supposedly why Eskimos have traditionally been able to eat a high-fat, high-cholesterol diet without succumbing to heart disease: because most of their foods come from the sea and so contain relatively large amounts of these important "Omega-3" fatty acids.

Sugar, caffeine, and alcohol are also no-no's on this diet. Sugar in particular poses a great deal of stress on the body and, therefore, should be totally eliminated without a moment's delay.[58] Indeed, excessive sugar intake can cause hypoglycemic (blood sugar-lowering) episodes which in turn can cause distressing psychological symptoms in the mind. Moreover, if this hypoglycemic cycle is repeated long enough, a chronic psychological disturbance can result which in turn makes it more likely that drugs will be resorted to in the quest for relief. A little bit of honey is okay, but it is important to realize that in excessive quantities honey is almost as bad as sugar. Artificial sweeteners are also okay in small amounts, but seeing as to how they are man-made chemicals with a toxicity all their own, they should be used sparingly, if at all. Indeed, a significant percentage of the population has been said to show a fundamental intolerance to Nutrasweet, a man-made chemical which allegedly turns into extremely toxic wood alcohol (methanol) in the body.

As far as caffeine is concerned, it has been shown to suppress the immune system to some extent. This of course presents an additional amount of stress to the body and so should be avoided whenever possible. Even more important, though, is the fact that regular coffee intake represents a bona fide addiction, and as we have already seen, in order to

---

57. It has been said that eating a single fish caught in the immediate waters surrounding Los Angeles pollutes the body with more DDT than one would otherwise consume in an entire LIFETIME!

58. Interestingly enough, it is the unnatural refining of sugar cane which gives white sugar many of its unhealthy characteristics. In its raw state several important nutrients appear with the sugar which make it much safer to consume. The most important of these nutrients is the trace element chromium, which aids sugar metabolism in the body by forming an essential part of the sugar-regulating substance known as Glucose Tolerance Factor. During the refining process, however, the beneficial chromium is stripped away, rendering the sugar much more toxic for the body.

successfully give up one addiction, it is imperative that we try to give up all other health-limiting addictions as well.[59] Again, this is because the presence of one addiction in the mind presents a fertile breeding ground for other addictions to grow and develop. Nevertheless, it is still quite possible to drink coffee on a moderate basis and yet not "gravitate" towards more serious addictions. The key word, of course, is moderation.

This principle of moderation applies to alcohol consumption as well. If a person can drink moderately (no more than an ounce or two a day), not much harm will result. Indeed, numerous studies have shown that an ounce or two of alcohol per day actually reduces a person's risk of heart attack and stroke.

The problem with most ex-addicts is the part about moderation. Most ex-addicts have a hard time being moderate about anything. For a good number of them, if they drink at all, they are going to drink until they get drunk. In these cases, alcohol needs to be avoided completely, because even one drink can be the beginning of a return to chemical slavery. Many former heroin addicts, for instance, begin drinking as a substitute for their narcotic, only to become alcoholics in the process. However, regardless of the type of drug you are trying to kick, it is important to realize that alcohol stimulates the addictive center of the brain and therefore "teases" the mind with the possibility of addiction, something the ex-addict definitely doesn't need any part of. Consequently, it is probably best for most ex-addicts to thoroughly avoid the use of alcohol whenever possible.

As always, the key word is moderation. If you are sure that you can be moderate with your drinking, then by all means go ahead and have a beer or two. But if you know you can't be moderate, then forget it. It simply isn't worth the tremendous amount of risk involved.

8.7 Vitamin and Mineral Supplementation

A balanced program of nutritional supplementation can go a long way towards alleviating the discomfort experienced during withdrawal. It can also help to put you in a state of maximal health once you've freed yourself from your drug habit, which in turn makes it less likely that you will go back to drugs looking for physiological relief.

---

59. The second worst withdrawal syndrome I ever had to contend with was from a serious habit of several cappuccinos a day! The worst of all was from a three-and-a-half-year cigarette habit.

The most important vitamin for easing withdrawal symptoms is undoubtedly vitamin C, or ascorbate. Vitamin C acts as a general detoxicant and free-radical scavenger, so it can provide tremendous help in returning a withdrawing body to a state of biochemical normality when it is used correctly.

In order to be effective in combating withdrawal, though, vitamin C must be taken in megadose amounts throughout the day. The best way to be assured of taking an optimal amount of ascorbate is to use the bowel tolerance method of dose titration. Bowel tolerance means taking enough of this vital nutrient in divided doses throughout the day to bring one almost, but not quite, to the point of having diarrhea. The idea here is that the body uses almost all of the vitamin C it is provided with until the point of near diarrhea is achieved. Thus, the concept of bowel tolerance is simply a way of adjusting your intake of the vitamin to suit your own bodily requirements.[60]

The best form of vitamin C to take to help alleviate the pangs of withdrawal is the buffered form put out by the Nutricology Corporation of San Leandro, California.[61] Formulated by Doctor Stephen Levine, one of the nation's leading orthomolecular researchers, this form of vitamin C is buffered with calcium, magnesium, and potassium salts. Such a buffered solution provides several benefits to the body: (1) It provides the body with a quality source of non-acidic vitamin C, which is easier on the stomach than regular vitamin C. (2) It provides an excellent source of the anti-stress minerals calcium, magnesium, and potassium, which are lost during the withdrawal process itself. (3) It helps to reduce the tremendous acidity of the blood which results from the withdrawal process.

When all three of these factors work together, a near miraculous biological result is typically seen in the withdrawing addict. A few minutes after taking 4 or 5 grams of this buffered C solution, one usually finds the vast majority of one's withdrawal discomforts to be rapidly dissipating. This effect is often so dramatic that it really needs to be experienced to be believed. It is as if one has been poisoned and the buffered C is the antidote for the poison!

---

60. As always, pregnant women should consult their physicians before embarking on megavitamin therapy to aid in the withdrawal process, since high doses of vitamins could possibly have an adverse effect on the growing fetus.

61. You can order Nutricology's Buffered C Powder and other nutritional supplements direct by calling the following toll-free number: (800) 545-9960; in California (415) 639-4572.

The creator of this remarkable substance, Doctor Stephen Levine, is the founder and research director of the Allergy Research Group/ Nutricology Corporation of San Leandro, California. He has shown that this buffered C mixture, which he developed to quell his own allergic symptoms, is also capable of reducing withdrawal discomforts from all sorts of addictions, ranging from heroin and cocaine addiction to marijuana and nicotine addiction. Again, though, bowel tolerance doses need to be maintained throughout the day in order for the preparation to be effective. For many addicts in the throes of withdrawal, huge doses may be regularly needed to achieve this effect. Indeed, a dose of 7 to 10 grams every hour may even be needed in some severely ill people.[62]

Although the buffered C complex alone may suffice for some people, others may want to use a more complete regimen of vitamin and mineral supplementation both during and after withdrawal. This is a sensible approach, as it gives the body all the biochemical tools it needs to overcome the withdrawal process. If you don't want to worry with taking a number of different pills, you may just want to take a single multiple-vitamin supplement. Nutricology's Multi Vi-Min is one of the most complete multi-vitamin preparations available at the present time.

In addition to a multiple vitamin, several additional nutrients can be taken for their ability to quiet down the nervous system during withdrawal. Niacin in particular should be taken frequently, since in relatively high doses it can act as a natural tranquilizer.[63] However, since high doses of niacin can cause a harmless though uncomfortable flushing of the skin (which usually disappears after a few doses), you should start out at around 100 mg three times a day and work up to around 1000 mg two or three times a day. Then, when the withdrawal process is over, a maintenance dose of 1000 mg a day will usually be sufficient. If the flushing proves to be intolerable, niacinamide can be substituted for the niacin, since it doesn't produce this flushing effect. Unfortunately, though, it doesn't seem to provide as much relief as niacin itself does.

One of the reasons why high doses of niacin can help to ease a person through withdrawal is that it appears to bind in the same area of the brain that Valium does. Thus, high doses of niacin often have a natural

---

62. At these doses, it is next to impossible to be constipated, since the buffered C mixture acts as a potent but harmless laxative.

63. High doses of niacin also help to lower blood cholesterol, so you may want to continue taking it indefinitely. Optimal cholesterol reduction occurs at around 3000 mg a day.

tranquilizing effect on the mind. This is one of the reasons why it has been used with such success in treating schizophrenics.

Another substance which is amazing in its ability to calm the nerves and promote sleep is the amino acid L–Tryptophan, which is a natural constituent of protein. In the brain L–Tryptophan gets converted into the neurotransmitter serotonin, which has a calming effect on the brain. This is why everyone gets so sleepy after eating Thanksgiving Day dinner—because turkey meat contains an unusually high amount of this essential amino acid.

One or two grams of L–Tryptophan should be a sufficient dose for inducing sleep. Because amino acids compete for entry into the brain, the Tryptophan should be taken on an empty stomach. It should also be taken with a gram or so of vitamin C and 100 mg or so of vitamin B-6, since these nutrients help with the conversion of Tryptophan into serotonin.

Vitamin B-5, or pantothenic acid, is a potent anti-stress vitamin which should also be taken in mega-doses during withdrawal. A dose of 1000 mg two or three times per day should be sufficient.

Vitamin B-6, or pyridoxine, is a vital constituent of many critical enzymes in the body; it also helps the nervous system deal with the stress of withdrawal. A dose of 50 to 100 mg twice a day should be sufficient.

Vitamin A, either in its pure form or in the form of its precursor, beta-carotene, should also be taken during withdrawal, both for its ability to strengthen the immune system and for its widely recognized ability to retard cancer growth. This is an especially important concern for the substance abuser, since many forms of drug abuse have carcinogenic effects on the body. Approximately 10,000 to 25,000 I.U.'s of either vitamin should be sufficient.[64]

Linoleic and linolenic acids are two extremely important fatty acids which should also be taken as supplements during withdrawal. They are "essential" fatty acids in the sense that the body cannot make them for itself; consequently, they must be consumed in the diet or taken as supplements. These Omega-6 fatty acids have an important function in stabilizing cellular membranes and in strengthening the immune system in general. Unfortunately, there are only a few good sources of these vital

---

64. You may want to take beta-carotene instead of vitamin A, since it is converted into vitamin A in the liver in accordance with bodily needs. Consequently, it is safer to take than vitamin A, which can become toxic if too much is taken. Beta-carotene also appears to have more anti-carcinogenic activity than vitamin A itself does.

nutrients. The best sources are Evening Primrose Oil and flaxseed oil. They can be bought either as free-standing oils, which can be used in salad dressings, or as capsules.

The only other nutrients which might need to be taken in greater-than-normal amounts are the antioxidant minerals zinc and selenium and vitamin E. Selenium in particular, along with vitamin E, is vitally important in neutralizing toxicities and beefing up the immune system. Around 200 mg of selenium along with 1000 I.U.'s of vitamin E should be sufficient. A total of around 25 or 50 mg of elemental zinc should also be optimal. But remember, you should be getting a healthy quantity of these nutrients in your multi-vitamin, if you choose to take one, so be sure to check their amounts before you start to take additional supplements. Too many vitamins can often be just as bad as too few![65] Selenium in particular can be toxic if too much is taken, so be careful not to exceed the recommended dosage.

Once the withdrawal process is completed, it is important to maintain a regular process of nutritional supplementation in order to keep the body and mind in optimal health. Significantly reduced dosages, particularly of the buffered C complex, will usually suffice once withdrawal is over. You will be able to see these reduced bodily requirements directly in a greatly reduced bowel tolerance level for ascorbate.

8.8 The Wonders of Exercise

Perhaps the most indispensable tool in coping with the pain and anxiety of withdrawal is a good exercise program. Absolutely nothing is as effective as exercise in dissipating the suffering which naturally accompanies the withdrawal process.

For me, running was the exercise of choice. Everytime I would begin to feel shaky from my withdrawal, I would go out for a ten- or fifteen-minute run around the neighborhood. When I would return, my suffering would be almost totally eliminated, at least for the time being. Although it would invariably return a few hours later, I simply did the same thing over and over again. It was a great way to relax while simultaneously getting into better physical and mental shape.

---

65. Fortunately, vitamin C and all of the B vitamins are water-soluble, so excessive quantities are usually flushed out in the urine.

CAUTION: Initiating a sudden aerobic exercise program can conceivably provide the stimulus for a heart attack or stroke, especially during the stress of drug withdrawal and especially if there is any pre-existing pathology in these areas. Consequently, it is an ABSOLUTE MUST that you consult a physician before undertaking any type of aerobic exercise program.

This regimen of running several times a day to quell my withdrawal anxiety was especially effective in helping me to get off of cigarettes, since the running acted to flush my poisoned lungs out with relatively clean air. (I say "relatively clean air" because the smog of Los Angeles was almost as bad as the cigarette smoke itself!) Although I tried to smoke a few puffs after my first couple of runs, it was a futile effort, because the running made me cough repeatedly until my throat and lungs were all achy and scratchy. Apparently, the running purified my lungs to the point that a subsequent challenge with toxic cigarette smoke was more than they could bear without my coughing violently. This was great because it made smoking totally incompatible with my running, i.e. I couldn't continue smoking if I wanted to run every day, because no one in their right mind would want to cough that violently again. Consequently, I chose to continue running, and my cigarette smoking automatically disappeared as a result.

The moral of the story is clear: if you are trying to give up nicotine or any other kind of addictive drug, you should begin some type of exercise program as soon as possible. Running is fine, but so is cycling, swimming, or traditional aerobics. Indeed, swimming may be the most complete aerobic exercise of all, since you use almost all of your muscles in the exercise process; it is also the easiest on the body.

Intense aerobic exercise can have other beneficial effects in a person's life besides making the withdrawal process easier to bear. For one thing, it will probably extend your life by making you less susceptible to degenerative disease. It will also help to improve your overall state of mind in three separate ways: (1) through a hyper-oxygenation of your brain tissue; (2) through a stimulation of "runner's high," due to the release of endorphins in your brain; and (3) through the sense of mastery and achievement that regular exercise gives an individual.

Finally, a regular aerobic exercise program can enable you to be slightly more liberal with your diet. The general rule is: the more intense your exercise regimen is, the more liberal you can be with your diet.[66] Regular exercise causes the "metabolic flame" within the body's cells to burn hotter and brighter, thereby allowing you to burn away any nutritional excesses more efficiently.

8.9 Distraction as a Method for Improving Tolerance to Withdrawal Pain

If you are feeling up to it, a particularly good way to increase your capacity to tolerate the pain of withdrawal is to immerse yourself in some activity that offers a lot of distraction. I did this many times by going on side trips to Disneyland, Santa Catalina island, and even to Hawaii. In fact, I was enrolled in college during my entire withdrawal process; although sitting still in class was a major effort, my obsessive struggling for good grades provided more than enough distraction to help minimize my conscious suffering on a day-to-day level.

Depending on how much sickness you can tolerate, you can go to a movie, a football game, or to a local park to help you take your mind off the withdrawal process. If you feel up to it and can afford it, a major vacation can perhaps be the most distracting activity of all. You'll be amazed at how much a given distraction will help you to take your mind off your withdrawal misery.

8.10 Avoiding Temptation

For many ex-addicts, the hardest part about staying clean is when they find themselves in situations where they used to smoke, drink, or take pills. The urge to give in during such periods of temptation can literally be overwhelming, especially when you are surrounded by friends who are still using drugs.

Ideally, your inner resolve to never use drugs again will be so strong that no amount of temptation will be enough to persuade you to break your abstinence. In my own case, I suffered so much that literally nothing was capable of persuading me to give in. Of course, this was because I never wanted to suffer like that again, no matter what. In addition, I was also acutely aware of the fact that a few minutes of pseudo-pleasure can never be worth days and weeks of pain and suffering.

---

66. Athletes can only be liberal with their diets to a certain point, because they too are susceptible to diet-induced degenerative diseases.

Unfortunately, though, the majority of people who give up drugs don't seem to possess this much willpower, largely because they haven't suffered enough. If this is the case with you, it pays to change your behavioral patterns completely so that tempting situations can be avoided as much as possible.

For example, if you are trying to kick a cocaine habit and your willpower is particularly weak, it would be foolish to go to a party where cocaine is the main attraction. Similarly, if you are trying to quit smoking pot and most of your friends are heavy pot smokers, it would be extremely prudent to find a new set of non-smoking friends; at the very least, you should avoid these pot-smoking friends until your willpower becomes strong enough for you to resist smoking even in their presence. (If your friends are true friends, they won't try to tempt you into breaking your abstinence, unless of course they don't know any better.)

A good way to make your abstinence more palatable is to save the money that you would normally spend on drugs and use it for something else that you really want, like a major trip or a new outfit. In this way you repeatedly reinforce yourself for quitting, and as any psychologist will tell you, reinforcing a behavior makes that behavior much more likely to continue.

8.11 New Treatment Modalities

According to Doctor Phyllis Saifer of Berkeley, California, several new treatment modalities now exist for easing the pain of drug withdrawal.

The most ingenious of these new treatment techniques is NeuroElectric therapy (NET), invented by Doctor Margaret Patterson, a Southern California surgeon. The idea behind NeuroElectric therapy is simple, yet profound. A small Walkman-like device is worn on the belt. This device transmits a tiny electric current to a special area behind the ears; somehow this current is able to greatly reduce the agony of drug withdrawal.

It has been hypothesized that NeuroElectric therapy is able to ease withdrawal pangs by stimulating the brain to produce its own tranquilizing chemicals, probably by harmonizing with the brain's own natural electrical rhythms. According to rock star Pete Townsend, "The treatment is effective for booze, cigarettes, barbiturates, cocaine, marijuana, you name it. There's a different frequency that works best for each kind of addiction."

It takes less than ten days to totally withdraw an addict in this manner, but then the *real* challenge begins. NeuroElectric therapy may be able to wean a person off of drugs, but it can't help him to stay off once he's totally clean; that, of course, is up to him.

Another novel treatment technique for easing withdrawal involves a procedure that has been used for thousands of years: acupuncture. With acupuncture the body's own tranquilizing and cleansing systems are stimulated by a series of tiny needles which are inserted at strategic points on the body. This may sound horribly painful and even ridiculous, but the fact of the matter is that there is virtually no discomfort involved in the procedure at all; moreover, it has been shown to be an extremely effective method for helping some patients to kick the habit.

A related technological innovation called "electro-acupuncture" is also being used both to aid in the process of withdrawal and to stabilize the individual once the withdrawal process is over. With electro-acupuncture, the natural meridians used by traditional acupuncturists are examined and treated using sensitive electrical fields hooked up to elaborate computer systems. Not only can diseases be detected at very early stages in the body's various organ systems, it can also be instituted to help bring the body back into balance (equilibrium) with itself. It has been hypothesized that electro-acupuncture treatments are able to help withdrawing addicts because they help to stimulate painkilling endorphin production in the brain.

Two new treatments for alcoholic craving have also been recently devised. One involves utilizing the amino acid glutamine to help restore the nutritional imbalance which supposedly causes alcoholic craving. A half a gram (500 mg) is recommended both before and after meals and at bedtime. The use of glutamine is almost always safe because it is a health-building nutrient which occurs naturally in food.

Lithium, the drug used to treat manic-depressive disorders, is also being used to treat alcoholic craving. According to Chicago physician Jan A. Fawcett, lithium doesn't exert its main effect by modulating the alcoholic's depression; it actually *suppresses* the urge to drink through a biochemical pathway not yet elucidated.

A recent study helps to confirm this unforeseen effect of lithium. Eighty-four long-standing alcoholics were used in the study. Seventy-five percent of the drinkers who were maintained on lithium were still off the bottle after eighteen months, while a full 100 percent of those who had stopped taking the drug relapsed! Clearly, the use of lithium in treating alcoholic craving is a major breakthrough and promises to be of great help in getting former alcoholics to stay off the bottle forever.

Antabuse, the drug which causes violent illness if any alcohol is consumed, may still be effective for some people, but in theory it doesn't even compare with glutamine and lithium, since it doesn't directly affect alcoholic craving at all. In addition, Antabuse often causes severe side effects which greatly reduce its overall effectiveness. A new drug, cyanimide, also causes a severe distaste for alcohol but doesn't cause the side effects. It is awaiting FDA approval.

The antihypertensive drug clonidine hydrochloride (brand name Catapres) has recently been shown to help ease withdrawal pangs from such narcotic drugs as heroin, morphine, and Percodan; it also seems to work with nicotine withdrawal as well. According to Doctor Janice Phelps in her book *The Hidden Addiction* (Little, Brown, and Company, 1986), studies at Yale University have revealed the use of clonidine to be an extremely effective way of quelling withdrawal symptoms in narcotics addicts.

Several other drugs are also being used to help ease withdrawal from severe cocaine addiction. Psychiatrist Mark Gold of Fair Oaks Hospital in Summit, NJ, a true pioneer in the field of substance abuse disorders, has successfully been using the drugs bromocriptine, imipramine, and desipramine to help ease cocaine withdrawal by restoring normal dopamine levels in the brain.

The tremendous high that users get from cocaine is apparently caused by the increased production of dopamine in the brain. However, the brain's natural stores of this critical neurotransmitter are rapidly exhausted by the repeated use of cocaine. It is this depletion which is largely responsible for both the addict's intense craving for the drug as well as for the serious depression which often follows an intense cocaine high.

Consequently, any drug which can help to increase dopamine levels in the brain should be able to help ease the notorious cocaine withdrawal syndrome, and this is precisely how bromocriptine, imipramine, and desipramine (the latter two of which are commonly used antidepressants) seem to work. The amino acids tryptophan and tyrosine are also being used to help restore normal neurotransmitter levels in withdrawing cocaine addicts.

Unfortunately, these novel treatment modalities offer only temporary help. Once the initial withdrawal period is over, it is up to the ex-addict to stay clean on his own. This is an incredibly difficult proposition for most ex-addicts, but it can be made a good deal easier if the life-style changes discussed in this book are seriously implemented on a day-to-day level.

The Use of Germanium as a Treatment for Cocaine Withdrawal

Epidemiologist Michael Weiner of San Francisco has put forth a novel theory about the nature of cocaine addiction. He believes that the addict's craving for cocaine is directly related to a mild state of hypoxia, or lack of oxygen, in the brain, along with a mild state of hypoglycemia, or low blood sugar. This hypoxia and hypoglycemia may be due to stress, a lack of exercise, poor circulation, or an inadequate diet. But since the brain is so exquisitely sensitive to even the slightest dip in oxygen or glucose levels within the blood, these deficiencies are subjectively experienced as being intensely unpleasant.

According to Weiner, though, cocaine has the remarkable ability to greatly increase both oxygen and glucose levels within the brain almost immediately. This restores normal brain functioning in the addict and thus makes him feel a whole lot better, at least temporarily.

Now, assuming that a deficiency of oxygen and glucose is what makes the addict crave cocaine, then restoring normal blood levels of these substances should largely alleviate the addict's craving. In his book *Getting Off Cocaine* (Avon Books, 1983), Weiner recommends a diet-and-exercise routine similar to the one described in this book as the best way to increase both oxygen and glucose levels in the brain.

However, the recent introduction of organic germanium in this country by Doctor Levine's Nutricology Corporation promises to make the cocaine addict's withdrawal process easier than ever. Germanium is an element on the Periodic Table that has semiconductor capabilities, which explains its widespread use in the electronics industry. It is a natural constituent of many foods, including garlic and shelf fungus, and it has been shown to be the primary active ingredient in the healing waters of Lourdes, France.

However, the most remarkable thing about germanium is its ability to increase the oxygenation of biological tissues. It is this unique characteristic which is supposedly responsible for the large number of miracle cancer cures which have been documented by Doctor Asai, a Japanese researcher, in his book *Germanium: Miracle Cure*, which is also available from Nutricology in California.

But if germanium can increase tissue oxygenation so effectively, and if the addict's craving for cocaine is caused at least in part by a lack of oxygen within the brain, then it logically follows that the daily use of organic germanium—which is essentially non-toxic—should significantly ease the addict's craving for cocaine. Although there are as yet no formal studies or treatment protocols on this subject, the liberal use of germanium in all forms of drug withdrawal appears to be eminently logical, since hypoxia is a component of virtually all withdrawal syndromes.

With this in mind, the withdrawing addict would do well to give organic germanium a try. A dose of 500 to 1000 mg a day should be sufficient.

8.12 In Case You Start to Feel Demoralized: A Word of Encouragement

Getting off an extensive drug habit can be one of the most difficult things a person will ever do in life. Moreover, during the pangs of withdrawal it is easy to lose sight of your overall purpose and to get demoralized by the seemingly endless pain and suffering that is experienced. If you get severely depressed during the withdrawal process, you might even begin to feel worthless and suicidal.

In case you start to feel this way, there is one thing you must never forget: from a scientific point of view, you are by far the most complicated and miraculous thing in the entire known universe! The neuro-circuitry of your brain, for example, is so unbelievably complicated that the computerized complexity of the space shuttle is like a child's play toy in comparison!

This fact has several critical implications for you. First, it means that you are an immensely important being, both to God and to the universe itself. To be sure, if God went to all the trouble of making you the most complicated object in the entire known universe, you MUST be exceedingly important to Him. But if this is so, then isn't it your Cosmic Duty to present the best possible "you" back to the universe? Of course it is, and it goes without saying that this can only be done in a drug-free state.

Second, your profound complexity and universal importance means that you can straighten yourself out, no matter how bad things may seem to be at the present time. If the quality of your inner design is without equal in the entire known universe, then you surely must be capable of getting out of a situation that you originally got your own self into!

Finally, the unsurpassed complexity of your inner design means that it is foolhardy indeed to try to improve things with drugs. God obviously knew what He was doing when He designed our minds the way He did, so how can we be so audacious as to assume that we can improve on His already Perfect Design? It would be like pouring whiskey into one of the space shuttle's main computer banks in an effort to improve its functioning! If you are feeling bad inside, it doesn't mean that you were designed in a faulty manner or that you need drugs—it means that there are certain things in your life which need to be appropriately dealt with. To be sure, if there is a short-circuit in the space shuttle's computer system, it doesn't make any sense to try to fix it by pouring whiskey into it!

Whatever you do, then, don't EVER fall into the trap of believing that you are worthless and unimportant, because as we have seen, there isn't a more important creature than you in the entire known universe! In case you should start to feel worthless anyway, you should re-read this section and then do your best to get your life back in order as soon as possible. Whatever you do, don't start taking drugs again in order to cover up your depressed mood; it only makes things worse.

Chapter 9

A STRATEGY FOR STAYING CLEAN FOREVER

In order to stay off of drugs forever, a person must do two things religiously:

1. Become as physically healthy as possible.
2. Find alternate methods for dealing with stress.

Concerning the first requirement, getting off of all drugs (including nicotine) is the single biggest thing you can do for optimizing your own physical health. However, if you also change your diet as described in the previous chapter, take regular supplements, and exercise vigorously at least three or four times a week, you will soon get in better shape than you've probably ever been in your entire life! If you actually reach this point of optimal health, you will be tremendously safeguarded against the possibility of a relapse, since you will be feeling better straight than you ever felt on drugs!

9.1 Dealing With Candida Infections

In the interest of attaining a state of optimal health you must be careful to treat any underlying infections if they happen to exist. This is due to the fact that there are several systemic infections which are known to greatly increase the likelihood that you will either crave drugs or alcohol.

Chief among these infections to avoid is infestation with the famous yeast germ Candida albicans. Although the Candida organism is a normal part of our intestinal flora, it can grow to bio-toxic levels when certain things in our lives go out of balance or when our immune system gets overtaxed. When this yeast overgrowth occurs, it can cause all sorts of systemic problems due to the production of many allergy-causing antigens and the production of the toxic chemical acetaldehyde (first-cousin to formaldehyde). Indeed, in certain people the yeast can ferment dietary sugars all the way into ethyl alcohol, producing a full-blown intoxication if the levels get high enough. In Japan—where this problem is seen quite often—it is called "the drunk disease."

The symptoms of chronic yeast overgrowth are often so intense and unpleasant that they can significantly increase the odds for a relapse in a recovered drug addict. These symptoms range all the way from gastrointestinal difficulties to full-blown psychiatric episodes. It is the psychiatric problems which most concern us in this book, since they are the ones which most encourage drug and alcohol abuse.

Chronic Candida overgrowth can cause severe depression, relentless headaches, frequent anxiety attacks, poor coping skills, a lack of coordination, a hypersensitivity to environmental chemicals, and just about any other psychiatric symptom imaginable! It has been hypothesized that these psychiatric symptoms are the result of yeast toxins which are interfering with normal neurotransmitter functioning in the brain.

With this in mind, what exactly causes Candida overgrowth in the body? First and foremost, certain prescription drugs are known to cause this problem. Broad-spectrum antibiotics in particular are Candida stimulators, because they wipe out the healthy intestinal flora in the colon which help to keep the yeast in check. Birth control pills are also notorious offenders, since they disturb the body's delicate hormonal balance so intensely (pregnancy does the same thing). Finally, cortisone and other corticosteroids also cause Candida overgrowth through a general weakening of the immune system.

Unfortunately, the recovered drug addict is an especially likely candidate for a Candida infection, since his immune system is already greatly compromised on two separate counts: (1) from years of taking immunosuppressive drugs and (2) from the severe biochemical stress of withdrawal in general. This immunosuppression in turn means that the body is no longer strong enough to keep the yeast germ in check.[67]

Indeed, once the Candida germ gains a slight foothold in the body, it initiates a vicious cycle where it becomes even more widespread in the tissues. Here's what happens: Once the immune system becomes compromised for whatever reason, Candida overgrowth is encouraged. This

---

67. Yeast overgrowth is just the beginning of a natural process which will eventually see our entire body rot away. We are literally surrounded by hungry germs on every side, and the only reason we aren't totally engulfed by them is that the immune defenders inside of us are still alive and well. However, just as soon as they let down their guard a tiny bit, they automatically allow these opportunistic germs to advance on us.

overgrowth allows the yeast to begin producing a wide variety of immunotoxic compounds, which further depress the immune system, which in turn allows the yeast to proliferate even more.

According to this biochemical scenario, it is quite likely that the stress of addiction and withdrawal can help to generate a severe Candida infection within the body. If and when this occurs, it usually ends up generating all sorts of unpleasant physical and psychological symptoms in the ex-addict, which in turn tempt him to self-medicate with more psychoactive drugs.

Perhaps this is one reason why there is such a high rate of recidivism among ex-addicts. Indeed, perhaps many of these individuals aren't as weak-willed as many would like to believe. Instead of simply giving in to the urge for a good time, perhaps many of these ex-addicts return to drug abuse as a last-ditch effort to deal with an inner physiological problem that their doctor was unable to properly deal with. If this is the case, then the ignorance of the traditional medical establishment is just as much to blame for the high recidivism rate among ex-addicts as the addicts themselves.

If you suspect that you may have a Candida infection, your first order of business is obviously to find a doctor who can properly diagnose and treat you. Fortunately, the modern physician now has at his disposal several potent ways of diagnosing a Candida problem, chief among them being a highly sensitive blood test (the CEIA exam) and a detailed medical history.

Unfortunately, though, not all doctors are familiar with the Candida germ; some even routinely deny its widespread importance in medicine. Thus, it is imperative that you see a physician who treats this problem on a regular basis. Most clinical ecologists and holistic practitioners now specialize in treating the yeast problem.

As far as prevention is concerned, there are basically only three things that you can do to optimize the chances that you will not be infected with the yeast germ. First, you must take extra special care to not take any antibiotics, birth control pills, or corticosteroids unless they are absolutely necessary. Second, you must eat the proper yeast-control diet.[68] The basics of this diet are no yeast, no refined sugars, no alcohol, no refined carbohydrates, the right nutritional supplements (vitamin C, selenium,

---

68. For a detailed explanation of this yeast-control diet, please refer to Doctor Crook's best-selling book *The Yeast Connection.*

and caprylic acid in particular), and plenty of lactobacillus-containing yogurt.[69] Finally, you must strive to get in optimal shape by regularly engaging in vigorous exercise and skilled relaxation.

The treatment for an ongoing Candida infection is basically the same as the preventative treatment, except for the addition of certain potent yeast-killing drugs. Nystatin is typically the first drug of choice,[70] but if the patient doesn't respond favorably to it, an even stronger drug called Nizoral is often used. The use of an anti-fungal herbal tea from Argentina called Taheebo or Pau d'Arco is also quite effective in controlling Candida overgrowth, as is the caprylic acid product already mentioned. A water-soluble vitamin A supplement is sometimes prescribed as well, since it has a favorable effect on the part of the bowel which is most damaged by the Candida germ.

If you are about to undergo Candida treatment with anti-fungal drugs, you should be aware of the fact that people often get worse during the first few days of drug treatment, due to the die-off of large numbers of yeast organisms and the release of their associated toxins. This is called the Herxheimer Reaction and it should be tolerated if at all possible, since it doesn't last very long (a few days at most).

When you finally recover, you should try to maintain your anti-yeast life-style indefinitely so that you won't suffer a relapse. In the meantime, your immune system will probably be getting stronger with each passing day, so after a few months you should be able to "cheat" a little on your anti-yeast diet and get away with it. However, you don't want to go too far, because it doesn't take much to initiate a relapse.

Another microorganism that can plague the ex-addict is the Epstein-Barr virus, which is the same virus that causes mononucleosis. Once you are infected with the Epstein-Barr virus, you are infected for life.[71] However, the symptoms produced by this virus vary tremendously from person to person, ranging from no effect at all in some people to a profound fatigue syndrome which can incapacitate even the strongest individuals. Most of the time, though, the Epstein-Barr virus appears to exert a constant, subclinical effect on a person's health through a suppres-

---

69. Lactobacillus organisms help to reinoculate the bowel with the healthy flora that act to keep the yeast constantly in check.

70. The name Nystatin is a type of acronym which tells the name of the state it was discovered in: NY–Stat-In!

71. A big difference between the Candida germ and the Epstein-Barr virus is that everyone has yeast cells living inside of them, whereas you have to be exposed to the Epstein-Barr virus in order to be infected by it.

sion of his immune system, which in turn makes him much more susceptible to other types of infections as well.

Fortunately, a daily program of healthful living seems to suppress the
Epstein-Barr virus into almost total inactivity. Like the Candida germ,
though, it is always waiting in the wings for you to become sufficiently
run down so that it can spring back into action and make you sick again.
Not surprisingly, mega-dose vitamin C therapy can combat these relapses
very effectively if it is taken properly.

It cannot be emphasized enough how important it is for you to maintain a state of optimal physical health in your body. This is because poor
physical health often produces poor mental health, and poor mental
health almost always forces you to look elsewhere for relief. Therefore,
by optimizing your physical health you can greatly reduce your inner
need to turn to drugs for relief.

This brings us to our final technique for staying off of drugs forever:
the optimization of our mental health. We need to get as mentally
healthy as possible if we want to avoid drug abuse, because there is an
inverse correlation between mental health and drug-taking behavior:
the more mentally healthy we are, the less likely we are to abuse drugs,
and conversely, the less mentally healthy we are, the more likely we are
to resort to a pattern of illicit drug use.

Unfortunately, though, achieving true mental health is exceedingly
difficult because there are so many complex factors which invariably
play into it, many of which lie beneath our level of conscious awareness.
The majority of these factors are psychological in nature, although as we
have seen, physical factors also play a prominent role in helping to
determine our overall state of mental health.

The first area we need to concentrate on in our quest for optimal
mental health is conflict resolution. We all tend to accumulate psychological conflicts and hangups as we grow through childhood and adolescence; the very process of growing up under less-than-perfect circumstances appears to endow us with them. Unfortunately, though, these
underlying conflicts act like little gremlins in our adult lives, effectively
sabotaging any attempt we make at true happiness. Consequently, the
first order of business once we reach adulthood should be to eliminate
these underlying hangups once and for all.

However, two things generally need to happen before we can set out to
resolve our inner conflicts: (1) we need to be convinced that these
conflicts exist, and (2) we need to know what they are comprised of and

where they are located. Answering the following questionnaire as truthfully as possible can help you to make these determinations.

A Questionnaire for Determining the Existence and Nature of Underlying Psychological Conflict

1. Are you resentful most of the time?
2. Do you get seriously depressed a little too often?
3. Do you feel unduly suspicious of other people's motives and behaviors?
4. Do you feel as if you would like to blow up in anger every so often? Do you feel that you would like to "settle the score" between you and a significant other, such as a parent or sibling?
5. Do you ever feel a sense of resentment or hostility towards your parents for how they treated you as a child or how they treat you now? If you had your druthers and could go back to being a child again, would you ask your parents to treat you any differently than they actually did?
6. Were you involved in many heated conflicts in your immediate family?
7. Have you ever thought about seeing a psychologist or a psychiatrist?
8. Whenever you are under an undue amount of stress, do you feel like getting drunk or taking drugs?
9. Have you ever thought about committing suicide?

If you answered "yes" to two or more of the above questions, the odds are very high that you have some type of deep-seated inner conflict which remains unresolved. And just like a reverberating electrical circuit which is unable to dissipate its overall amount of energy, an unresolved psychological conflict will continue to produce an unhealthy amount of negative emotional stress in your life until you get rid of it once and for all.

The questions you answered "yes" to on the above questionnaire also indicate the general area of conflict in your life. A well-trained therapist can help you to explore these areas in more detail.

At this point an interesting question suddenly presents itself: If your everyday experience really is being disturbed by some type of unresolved emotional conflict in your mind, then how come you aren't aware of it? The answer, of course, goes back to Freud's concept of the unconscious. The unconscious is that part of the mind which lies just beneath the level of conscious awareness. It is the "emotional dungeon" into which we have unknowingly dumped all our unwanted thoughts, memories, and feelings that we have accumulated over a lifetime. Because they are housed in our unconscious, we aren't aware of their presence by definition.

As Doctor Arthur Janov explains in his pioneering work THE PRIMAL SCREAM, the mind automatically represses into the unconscious all those thoughts and feelings which the ego deems are too painful for conscious experience. In infants this process of repression is a critical survival instinct, because it helps them to tolerate an otherwise intolerable situation: that of being born in a totally helpless and defenseless condition in an imperfect world which can never cater perfectly to their every developmental need.

That is to say, because the infant hasn't yet developed an adequate psychological defense system, it can't protect itself from emotional pain the way adults can. It is emotionally naked, so to speak, so it cannot bear to fully experience the pain of feeling unloved and unattended to; if it did, it would die from the tremendous onslaught of pain.[72] Therefore, when the infant actually begins to experience this pain, it does what comes naturally: it automatically represses it to the mysterious realm of the unconscious.

All babies repress pain to some degree. Due to the natural imperfections which are an inherent part of childraising, all babies experience emotional pain which is sufficiently intense to trigger the repressive process. It doesn't take an openly abusive situation to generate this pain—even the best of parents unknowingly subject their babies to these pain-generating circumstances from time to time. It simply isn't humanly possible for parents to anticipate their baby's every developmental need in such a way that it is catered to before the baby feels uncomfortable.

In other words, it isn't always the situation itself which is to be blamed for the infant's experience of pain; it is the unbelievable vulnerability of the defenseless infant which makes it so extraordinarily sensitive to its environment, even when it is under the best of care. Consequently, it appears as though the complications which arise from habitual repression are an integral part of the human condition.

Eventually, this psychological process of repression becomes a condi-

---

72. Some theorists believe that the phenomenon of crib death is actually a failure of the repressive process in the infant's brain. According to this theory, when the repressive act fails, a flood of emotional pain rapidly overwhelms the infant's defenseless ego and he dies as a result.

tioned habit in the infant. From this point onward, every time the growing child experiences an emotional pain which is too much for him to comfortably bear, he automatically does his best to repress it into his unconscious. This process of repression even continues into adulthood, where it enables the individual to conveniently dispose of thoughts and feelings he would rather not have to face.

Of course, some of us are more effective at this repressive process than others. Those who are most effective at it are generally the overly repressed "anal-retentive" personality types who are almost totally without conscious feeling. On the other hand, those who are least effective at it are the overly emotional, neurotic personality types who are literally overwhelmed with feeling. Since they are unable to effectively repress their unwanted emotions and since they don't know how to properly get rid of them, they are condemned to suffer indefinitely under their loathsome presence.

Unfortunately, though, all the years of aborted emotional pain that we have conveniently repressed away do not disappear. On the contrary, they remain in the unconscious in full force, perfectly preserved in their original, pristine form. But they don't just sit there in an idle, purposeless fashion. Rather, they are constantly struggling to be released into the conscious mind, because their goal is always to complete the original aborted experience in all its original intensity.

Predictably, though, the conscious mind is scared silly by the possibility that these repressions will gain access into conscious awareness. After all, this is why the mind repressed these pains to begin with: because it felt that they were too threatening to be fully experienced. So what does the conscious mind do? It mobilizes all of its available energy into its repressive ability so that it can keep its repressions buried at all cost.

Naturally, though, this inner battle between the conscious mind and the unconscious mind exacts a heavy price: it causes the personality to be built around the "vital lie" of repression, which in turn also causes the mind to be distorted into the psychopathologies of neurosis and psychosis.

When I say that these unconscious repressions cause the personality to be built around the vital lie of repression, I simply mean that in order to keep these unconscious pains adequately repressed, we must constantly lie to ourselves about both their existence and their importance in our lives. Hence, our very personalities are designed to deny, or to lie about, the truth of our inner pain.

Moreover, this inner split between the conscious and the unconscious mind causes an unhealthy split in our underlying character structure as well. Since we are constantly fighting an inner battle between repression and unrepression, we are effectively divided against ourselves on a deep psychological level. However, as the Bible tells us, anything which is divided against itself is bound to fail; this is undoubtedly why we tend to sabotage our own selves so often in our day-to-day lives. To be sure, as long as we continue to fight an endless battle of psychological repression, we really are our own worst enemy.

Our inner conflict is evident in just about everything we do. It is also evident in our emotional reactions to things. This is why we tend to get so inexplicably angry or depressed from time to time: because certain events in the real world tend to trigger our unconscious feelings of anger and sadness which we have retained from childhood.

Worst of all, the tremendous psychological pressure that is generated by years of unconscious repressions all struggling for release at the same time presents a formidable repressive task for the conscious mind. Consequently, in order to keep these old pains adequately repressed, a truly heroic amount of psychological effort must be expended during each and every waking moment.[73] When this pressure exceeds a certain critical level, it automatically acts to distort the conscious mind into the psychopathologies of neurosis and psychosis.

An analogy may help us to better understand this phenomenon. Imagine a tea kettle with water in it that is being heated on a stove. Further imagine that there isn't a hole in the kettle which is big enough to allow an adequate venting of the excess steam that is produced. Now if the kettle continues to be heated, the excessive pressure will eventually act to distend the kettle at its weakest point; it may even cause it to blow up if the pressure gets to be high enough.

In the same way, the unconscious repressions which most of us possess also generate a tremendous amount of pressure on our conscious mind. However, because the conscious mind is constantly fighting back with the process of repression, it doesn't allow a sufficient venting of this excessive pressure. The result is a "distension" of the conscious mind at its weakest point, which in turn produces what we call neurosis and psychosis.

The human mind is a curious thing. It demands to fully experience

---

73. This is undoubtedly why neurotics feel so tired all the time—because they are unknowingly using most of their available energy in the repressive process.

each and every little thing that ever happens to it, regardless of the amount of pain involved. The process of repression interferes with this demand by halting a given conscious experience whenever it becomes too painful. In the process of doing so it splits the experience up and channels the most painful part into the unconscious mind, where it remains unchanged from then on. It's as if the mind has the ability to temporarily stop emotional "explosions" by freezing them before they get too painful; the unfinished explosion is then automatically consigned to the unconscious mind for subsequent storage. However, like any natural process which is interrupted before it is finished, the tendency is always for the process to become completed. Repressed experiences are the same way; they too are striving for completion—and therefore resolution—by constantly struggling for release into the conscious mind.

In this sense the psychological dynamics surrounding the process of repression appear to be a spiritual form of the physical law which says that energy can neither be created nor destroyed, only changed in form. Now a painful emotional reaction to a given event is certainly a kind of energy. Once it is formed, though, the most painful part of it cannot be destroyed, regardless of how convenient it is for the conscious mind; it can only change form into an unconscious repression. Even so, it never loses its original power (which would be tantamount to a destruction of energy); it simply expresses its power in a subtle, hidden manner. The psychopathologies of neurosis and psychosis derive their power from this unconscious source.[74]

All of this psychological theorizing may be fine and well, but exactly what does it have to do with our goal of remaining drug-free forever? The tie-in is simple. As long as we have a significant number of unconscious repressions which are struggling for release, we are going to be constantly experiencing a tremendous amount of psychological stress, AND IT IS PRECISELY THIS PSYCHOLOGICAL STRESS WHICH MAKES US MOST APT TO USE DRUGS FOR RELIEF.

From a clinical point of view, the drug addict (especially the narcotics addict) is having a tremendous amount of trouble managing his repressions. In fact, without his daily fix, he can't seem to keep his repressions at bay at all.[75] This is why he needs his drugs so desperately—not

---

74. The devil can be thought of as being an external personification of our unconscious repressions. Certainly, both the devil and our repressions cause us to behave in all sorts of self-destructive ways. Both are extremely subtle and both follow us around wherever we go.

75. Biochemically speaking, most illicit drugs act to kill psychological pain in one way or another.

because he likes to get high so often, but rather because it is the only way he can keep his extremely fragile psychological world from crumbling down.

Now if most addicts use drugs because they are having trouble with their repressions, it follows that the best way to reduce their desire for these drugs is to somehow get rid of their repressions. Unfortunately, though, this is much easier said than done. We can't just go to a brain surgeon and request that our psychological repressions be removed from our unconscious! On the contrary, there appears to be only one way to get rid of these repressions once and for all, and that is by allowing ourselves to finish feeling them in all their original intensity. After all, an emotional repression is simply an aborted feeling, so in order to get rid of it we first need to finish feeling it.

Unfortunately, though, this is an extremely tall order for most people, since it requires them to face a part of themselves that they're absolutely terrified of. It is also difficult because it inevitably involves a tremendous amount of emotional upheaval in their lives, and most people are already up to their ears in problems and responsibilities. Worst of all, it's not a one-shot deal which only takes a day or two; it's a long, drawn-out process which can take months or even years![76] Understandably, most people are unwilling to make such an extended emotional sacrifice.

However, it isn't as if you can voluntarily choose to do this emotional purging when you're feeling fine. You can't. Due to the unique character of the purgative process, you have to feel driven to purge yourself. But the only way you can feel driven in this manner is when there is a significant degree of "leakage" in the repressive process. This is why drug addicts and mental patients may be the closest of all to true mental health: because they are the ones who are closest to their own repressions. This is why these individuals suffer so intensely—because they are standing right up against their own repressed feelings. As long as they resist letting go, however, they will continue to suffer indefinitely, because suffering is how the mind responds when we oppose our repressions.

Although the psychological purging we are describing here is absolutely necessary for an ideal state of mental health, it is highly impractical most of the time. And for all but the most disturbed people, it isn't even necessary to do so in order to be able to stay off of drugs. A certain

---

76. The reason for this, of course, is that we can only consciously integrate a single feeling at a time without being overwhelmed, and most of us have hundreds of repressed feelings to deal with.

amount of neurotic "pollution" can continue to exist in a person's mind without too much harm, and as long as one's repressions remain sufficiently buried, one can continue to live a relatively normal life indefinitely. Even if there has already been a drug-induced weakening of the repressive process in the mind, one can still use the various physical and mental treatments discussed previously to help fortify one's repressive ability so that a greater degree of psychic equilibrium can be achieved. However, for the psychological cripple who can't seem to cope without drugs, the only solution may be a radical purging of his unconscious storehouse of repressed pain.

Fortunately, there are several clinics around the world which specialize precisely in this form of "implosive" psychotherapy. Doctor Arthur Janov's Primal Institute in Los Angeles was the first clinic to initiate this type of radical treatment procedure. His best-selling book, *The Primal Scream*, eloquently documents the scientific rationale behind Primal Therapy and describes the actual process of therapy in detail.

Unfortunately, though, Primal Therapy is both prohibitively expensive and difficult to get accepted into. Other less expensive clinics claim to practice Primal Therapy, but it is hard to tell how reputable they really are. If you are sufficiently motivated, though, it is possible to carry out the basics of Primal Therapy in the privacy of your own room, but you should first be aware of several things before you actually try to do so. First, you should realize that any attempt at a self-directed Primal Therapy session can be dangerous, because it can open up a type of Pandora's box within the mind by partially loosening one's repressions; this in turn can end up leading to an initial worsening of symptoms if the feeling isn't properly integrated. Secondly, for most people self-directed Primal Therapy isn't even possible in the first place, because it totally goes against the natural grain of our conscious inclinations. Few people indeed are willing to face their deepest pains and fears unless they are literally forced to do so by a Primal Therapist.

Ideally speaking, then, it is best to see a Primal Therapist or a traditional therapist who can help you to get in touch with your innermost feelings. If you are unable to do this and yet feel that you can make contact with your repressed feelings entirely on your own (or with a friend, perhaps), you might want to take a shot at a self-directed Primal experience.

Here's what to do. The next time you start to feel extremely depressed (the blacker the mood, the better), try to find a private room where you can isolate yourself for several hours at a time. Be sure and have some Kleenex on hand. If you have a close friend, it may be helpful to have her sit with you during your therapeutic "session."

Once you are situated, dim the lights and try to begin focusing on the exact nature of your inner discomfort. Describe the feeling you are having in detail, either to yourself or to your friend, if you have one there with you. Concentrate solely on the feeling, not just so you can understand it, but so you can actually feel it.

One of the best ways of catapaulting yourself into an inner feeling is to describe an emotionally charged experience that you have recently had. For example, if you saw a movie or had a dream recently that made you feel bad, describe exactly what it was about the movie or dream that made you so sad. As always, the goal is to eventually reach an old feeling that you had as a child towards your parents.

Some people find it helpful to visualize their parents' faces when they're trying to get "into" a feeling. Others find that they can propel themselves into a feeling by actually calling out to their parents. If your feeling involves an argument with your mother or father, describe how the argument made you feel. If you felt like screaming to your parents during the argument but never actually did, then by all means take the liberty to do so during your self-appointed therapy session. This verbal replaying of the original argument should help to catapult you into the underlying feeling. As you get closer and closer to your old feeling, try to "let go" completely. Don't worry, nothing horrendous will probably happen to you beyond the experience of a few tears. Remember: you've first got to lose control before you can gain control—you've got to lose control of your repressions before you can gain control of a healthy and relatively unrepressed personality.

Once you have interjected yourself into the old feeling, feel it for all it's worth. Cry till you can't cry anymore. Wail till you can't wail anymore. And don't worry about how long it takes; the longer you cry, the more you cleanse yourself of your inner repressions.[77]

When you are finally finished an hour or two later (sometimes longer, sometimes shorter), you will be amazed at how much different you'll feel. If you have made a successful connection to an old feeling, you will probably end up feeling more relaxed than you've ever felt in your

---

77. When the Bible speaks about "purifying your heart," it is probably referring to this very process of emotional purging.

entire life, because a major source of psychological pressure that you've been carrying around since childhood will have finally been dissipated forever. You may also begin to be flooded with dozens of insights about the true origin of your past and present behavior.

If you continue with your psychological purging on a regular basis, you may find that seemingly unrelated things like allergies and asthma may also spontaneously begin to clear up. The reason for this is not far to seek: each reduction in the mind's unconscious "pool" of pain reduces the overall amount of strain in the mind, which in turn reduces the overall amount of strain in the body. This lessening of bodily strain can reveal itself in a number of different ways, such as in a lessening of muscular tension or an overall increase in energy.

Interestingly enough, the worse you happen to be feeling, the easier it will be for you to get into your old feeling, because feeling bad is usually an indication of some type of repressive "leakage." This is why the withdrawing drug addict and the chronic depressive are in the best position of all to feel their repressed pains—because they are so extraordinarily close to them.[78] In the case of the withdrawing drug addict, the biochemical effect of drug withdrawal naturally causes a weakening of the mind's "repressive lid," which in turn puts the suffering addict right up against his inner pain.

Indeed, it is the partial liberation of his unconscious repressions which is responsible for much of the suffering seen in the withdrawing addict. However, since these repressions are never fully felt, they are never fully resolved; they just "hang around," so to speak, and make the addict miserable until he either goes back to drugs for relief or gets enough psychological strength to repress them again. This is perhaps the largest single cause of recidivism in ex-addicts.

Fortunately, this problem of unconsciously motivated recidivism can be headed off during the initial withdrawal process before it ever gets to the point of causing a relapse. The withdrawing addict simply has to do his best to feel his psychological pains whenever they're stimulated by the withdrawal process. If he can do this during the entire withdrawal procedure, he will have succeeded at doing something very few other people down through history have ever done: purge themselves of their

---

78. This is also why Janov believes that many of these people are closer to true mental health than many so-called "normal" people are: because they are so much closer to purging themselves of their repressed pains.

inner repressed pains. Indeed, in my own theology I claim that this purging of the unconscious is one of the ultimate goals of Christianity, and that if it isn't done in this world, it will most definitely take place in the next world, in either Purgatory or Hell itself! So, what we are talking about here is an extremely important process, and the withdrawing addict is perhaps the best equipped of all of us to accomplish this laudable goal.

But what if you want to optimize your mental health without going through such a lengthy emotional ordeal? Is there anything else that you can do to maximize your mental health with a minimum of time and effort? There certainly is, and we've already mentioned most of them! What I'm referring to, of course, are the health-building techniques we've already discussed in the last two chapters. Exercising vigorously several times week, eating the right foods, taking the right supplements, and getting treated for allergies and Candida infections can do wonders for improving your overall mental health.

However, there is one additional technique that you can learn which will greatly improve both your physical and your mental health: skilled relaxation training. Skilled relaxation training only takes twenty minutes or so once or twice a day, but it can greatly reduce the harmful effects of stress in your life, and this in turn will automatically reduce your chance for a relapse. You can learn how to perform biofeedback training, meditation, yoga, and other relaxation techniques from a variety of sources, including psychologists, counselors, books, and cassette tapes.

Another effective way of dealing with stress is to prevent it from happening in the first place, if you possibly can. Because you are largely the master of your own fate, you can significantly lower your overall stress level if you consciously make the decision to do so, and a lower stress level automatically means that you are at less risk for a relapse. So, if the source of your stress is an unhappy work environment, change jobs! If you don't like your friends anymore, find others! If you don't like where you are living, move! If you are miserable at home, get professional help, and do your best to improve the relationships in your life; after all, life is much too short to waste it being unhappy at what you are doing.

By the same token, if your children are causing you problems, look for the source of the trouble and try to deal with it the best way you can. Parents are generally responsible for causing much of the suffering in their children's lives, so do your best to change your parenting behavior for the better if you possibly can. It may even require that you seek professional help for awhile, but when it's all over you'll be glad you did. Your children will be better for it, your relationship with them will improve, and your overall stress level will undoubtedly diminish.

A significant amount of stress is generated simply by living a temporary life in a temporary world. This is called "existential stress," and we all suffer from it to varying degrees. We all fear death to some extent, we all need something to live for, and we all need something to give our lives meaning. This is the function of religion. Having a comfortable relationship with one's Creator can go a long way towards easing the existential anxiety in one's life; it can even help you to completely eliminate your existential anxieties if you become particularly well advanced in your religious development.

Of course, this doesn't necessarily mean that you have to become a traditional Christian like Mrs. Jones down the block or like so and so on Channel 44. On the contrary, true religion is an extremely personal thing between an individual and his Maker, so if you are sincere, you can practice this type of religion in the privacy of your own room. At the same time, though, regularly attending church services can go a long way towards raising your religious awareness and heightening your overall psychological development.

In conclusion, it is well within anyone's power to stay off of drugs forever if the proper preventative measures are taken. Do yourself a favor—act on them—and you will enjoy a much healthier and happier life because of it!

Chapter 10

WHAT SOCIETY CAN DO
TO HELP PREVENT DRUG ABUSE

In this book we have concentrated on the free will of the individual in our quest to help reduce drug abuse in our society. To be sure, it is the individual and the individual alone who has ultimate power over the use of drugs. Thus, if an individual sincerely desires to use drugs, all the laws in the world aren't going to stop him. Similarly, if a person is determined to not use drugs, all the persuasion in the world isn't going to force him to do so.

Nevertheless, there is still a great deal that society can do to help prevent drug abuse. It may not have ultimate power in combating the use of drugs,[79] but it can still help to persuade the individual to "just say no" whenever he is tempted with a drug-using opportunity.

There are a variety of ways of doing this. The most effective and cost-efficient way is mass education: if people are shown exactly what drugs can do to them, they will be far less likely to want to use drugs themselves. The key to this type of education, though, has to be with making the information as personal and as relevant to the individual's life as possible. The best way to do this is by involving the individual in some type of direct experience of a drug-induced casualty so that he can actually feel how bad it is to get messed up on drugs.

A field trip to a drug detoxification center would be a good start, since it shows in no uncertain terms how horrible it is to be enslaved to a chemical habit. If such a field trip isn't possible, a videotape depicting the many horrors of drug-induced mental illness may suffice.

Back in the late seventies the "Scared Straight" program of criminal deterrence operated on a similar rationale. It brought kids directly to prison for a first-hand view of what they have to look forward to if they opt to choose a life of crime. The prisoners who volunteered to scare the

---

79. We must never be deluded into believing that the ultimate power in combating drug abuse lies with the government. It lies with the individual, and nothing short of 1984's Big Brother is going to change that.

kids straight were particularly effective in this regard. They scared the devil out of just about everyone who came to the prison; they even scared the people at home who were watching the show on TV!

This raises an additional point. Although a first-hand experience of a given tragedy may be the most effective way of deterring behavior, videotapes can also be extremely effective if they are done properly. Consequently, a well-done series of videotapes depicting the real-life horrors of drug abuse should be quite helpful in discouraging the use of drugs—both in adults and school-age children—because anything which helps to reduce the overall appeal of drugs will simultaneously help to reduce drug-taking behavior.

Although it is unlikely to ever be seriously implemented on a large scale (for obvious reasons), one of the most effective tools for preventing drug abuse would be a videotape or an actual witnessing of an autopsy of a drug overdose victim, especially if it is accompanied by the passionate testimony of a well-known ex-addict. For once the potential abuser sees exactly what can happen to him if he chooses to get overly involved with drugs, he is much less likely to begin using them; if he is already an abuser, he is much more likely to quit entirely.

This is due to a behavioral phenomenon known as operant conditioning. In operant conditioning, the individual's behavior is primarily determined by its anticipated consequence; this is why people don't jump in front of cars: because they can anticipate the probable consequence of doing so and they don't want to get run over and killed! In the same way, if a person can be convinced that there is a substantial likelihood that he will end up on an autopsy table if he chooses to use drugs, he will understandably be much less likely to use them. One of the best ways of convincing a person in this manner is to have him actually witness the autopsy of a drug overdose victim. Although such an individual may feel that his drug use will never get that far out of hand, the utter horror of seeing what could happen to him may be enough to get him to stop taking drugs once and for all.[80] There's certainly nothing like realistic fear to motivate people to change!

The classroom can also be an effective arena for drug abuse education, especially for school-age children. In order to be successful, though, such a class needs to be taught correctly and in a non-moralizing fashion

---

80. The idea here is to use the outright horror of witnessing an autopsy to compensate for the relatively low probability that such a grisly fate will happen to any one individual.

by the right person. Ideally, the teacher of such a class would be a sensitive and caring individual who has already been burned by drug abuse himself.

I cannot overemphasize how important it is for the teacher of a drug abuse class to have the "right" personality. This is because for most kids, the personality of a given teacher is more important than the actual subject that is getting taught. Thus, if the drug abuse teacher is admired and respected by the students, he is MUCH more likely to get them to seriously listen to his message. Conversely, if the teacher is seen as being an ignorant "square," the kids won't believe a word he says, and they may even use drugs outside of class in order to spite him.

If possible, the teacher of this type of drug abuse class should be available 24 hours a day for his students in case they need to talk about drugs outside of class. Such confidential meetings could go a long way towards establishing an effective buffer between the students and a life of drugs. Certainly, students should be able to get in touch with someone they trust and respect if they want to talk about things outside of class. Unfortunately, most students have no one at all to talk to about their potential drug use, so they have nowhere to turn when the temptation to use drugs suddenly presents itself.

Another way that society can begin making a serious dent in the drug problem is through heavy advertising. It is a well-known fact that clever and strategic advertising can make people buy or do almost anything. And when we consider the fact that children—the number one target audience for drug abuse education—represent the single largest proportion of daily television viewers, we suddenly have at our disposal an incredibly powerful weapon for fighting drug abuse at its very source: inside the individual. We can literally bombard young children with extremely persuasive anti-drug commercials on their own level, so that we can condition them into despising drugs before they even get to kindergarten.

A great way to strengthen the persuasiveness of these anti-drug commercials for both kids and adults alike is to use a well-known movie star to deliver the message. Stars automatically lend credence to whatever they say on the air because of the tremendous amount of respect they receive in this country.

To their credit, MTV (Music Television) has also jumped on the anti-drug bandwagon with their "RAD" series of commercials, which stands for "Rock Against Drugs." In these RAD commercials, world-famous rock stars, such as Bon Jovi and Mr. Mister, come right out and tell the viewing audience that drugs are for losers. This of course has an exceedingly powerful effect on viewers of all ages, but especially on young viewers, who are still involved in idol worship and who are thus still extremely malleable. Because these rock stars are so widely admired and are even worshiped by the teens in our society, their anti-drug messages carry an enormous amount of weight. The unspoken message seems to be that if the "coolest" members of our society are coming out against drugs, then drugs really and truly must be for losers. This in turn has the effect of strongly discouraging drug use in our youth. The musicians who participate in these "RAD" commercials are therefore to be commended for their heroic stance on this all-important issue.

Subliminal messages offer an even more sophisticated method of instilling an anti-drug bias deep within the television viewer's unconscious mind. A subliminal message is an imperceptible subconscious suggestion which is buried in either the audio or the video portion of a movie or television show. Incredibly, these subliminal messages have been shown to be capable of doubling the frequency of certain behaviors—such as eating popcorn in movie theaters—even though they are never consciously perceived by the viewer. Thus, it is conceivable that subliminal messages which discourage drug abuse could be strategically placed in various commercials and television shows, thereby producing an unconscious anti-drug stance in the television viewer's mind.

On the down side, though, using subliminal messages to fight drug abuse smacks of totalitarian mind control, so it probably will never be used for this purpose in this country. Although in this case it would be used for a good end, who's to say that it won't be used again for a much more ominous purpose in the future, such as paying homage to Big Brother?

On a more global level, fighting international drug trafficking at the source may be of some use, but it will always be a mixed blessing. On the one hand, federal narcotics officers are making bigger and bigger busts every day, but even so they are only scratching the surface of the huge international drug trade. For every pound of marijuana that is seized by customs authorities, many more pounds actually get through, and there doesn't seem to be much more that can be done about it.

At the same time, the billions upon billions of dollars that are spent trying to secure our nation's borders could be better spent on drug abuse education and on programs to end poverty, which is undoubtedly one of the biggest causes of drug abuse in this country. Indeed, if the individual's inner desire for drugs is the true problem, and if poverty is one of the leading causes of this desire, doesn't it make more sense to spend the DEA's billions on social programs to end poverty instead of on an international drug war that we can never win?

It is a futile battle: no matter how many drug shipments are intercepted in transit, those individuals who still want to take drugs will find a way to procure them. It is the classic economic law of supply and demand: as long as there is a demand for drugs in this country, there will always be a supply to fill it, no matter what the government does. Prohibition is the perfect example. Even though the government banned the sale of alcohol back in the thirties, illegal channels for alcohol production and distribution opened up almost immediately. The same sort of situation exists today. The DEA will never be able to significantly reduce drug use in this country by stopping international drug trafficking. And even if they could, it would be so enormously expensive that it would be totally impractical.

I'm not advocating legalization, mind you; I'm just trying to show the limits of prohibition and the direction in which we ought to direct the majority of our anti-drug efforts. Legalization is obviously not the answer because it would undoubtedly flood our society with even more addicts and other drug casualties, at least temporarily. It would also give a deadly stamp of approval to the highly impressionable youth of our country, who definitely don't need another reason to use drugs. While it may reduce the financial incentive of international drug traffickers, it does so at too high a price: the health and safety of our country's population. Indeed, the simple fact of the matter is that the illegal nature of hard drugs is a powerful deterrent for millions of people, many of whom would otherwise be confirmed narcotics addicts if the drugs were freely available.

In a society where drugs are illegal, there are two forms of deterrence: the destructive effect of the drugs themselves and the legal penalties which are levied on those who are caught using drugs. In a society where drugs are legal, on the other hand, there is only one primary form of deterrence: the destructive effect of the drugs themselves. Unfortunately, there are millions of people who won't learn how destructive drugs really are until their lives are totally ruined by them.[81] Consequently, we should keep hard drugs illegal, because when it comes to self-destructive poisons that people feel driven to take, the more forms of deterrence, the better.

The only way that we are going to be even modestly effective in reducing drug abuse in this country is by going to the true source of the problem: not the coca fields of Latin America, but the individual drug abuser's own inner desire for drugs. This is where education can play the biggest role in effecting change. It certainly costs a heck of a lot less to educate a person than it does to try to wage an all-out war on drug smuggling; it is also far more feasible and cost-effective as well. There's no doubt about it: a million dollars can be much better spent on educating a whole nation of people than on trying to intercept a few international drug shipments!

As far as routine drug testing is concerned, several points can be made. For one thing, it seems pointless and hypocritical to test only for illegal drugs on the job, since alcohol can cause just as many problems in the workplace as other drugs can. However, testing for drugs and alcohol clearly won't do for many companies, since such a large number of high-level executives drink on a daily basis, especially during lunch. If the corporate intent is to prevent drug abuse and to screen out as many drug-impaired people as possible, drug testing can act as an effective deterrent, but this still leaves alcohol users unscathed. However, if job performance is our primary criterion for judgment, it is both pointless and hypocritical to test for drug abuse without simultaneously testing for alcohol use as well.

At the same time, though, there are many jobs which absolutely require a sober mind, such as those involving public safety. In these instances it makes sense for the employer to routinely test for the ability to perform in an optimal fashion, but not only in terms of drug and alcohol abuse. There are many other factors which can also impair performance on the job; depression and anxiety attacks are two prime examples. Hence, if job performance is the issue, then all the factors which can potentially reduce performance should be properly addressed.

After all, the only issue which should truly matter to our corporate

---

81. In this sense many individuals are just like the laboratory rat who would rather push a bar for cocaine instead of food; both tend to consume their drug of choice repeatedly until they eventually die from their addiction.

leaders is the ability to perform one's job in a competent fashion. If an employee can do so, then it rightfully should be none of the employer's business whether or not he uses drugs or alcohol in his spare time. After all, the majority of Americans use mind-altering drugs at some point in their lives; does this mean that they should all lose their jobs because of it?

On the other hand, the drug-testing employer seems to be assuming that an employee who uses serious drugs at night and/or on the weekends is more likely to be impaired on the job than one who does not. There is a certain amount of truth to this assumption, because few drugs completely wear off overnight; moreover, people who take drugs at night and on weekends are also more likely to take them on the job. At the same time, though, by law the individual must be given a certain amount of privacy in his home life. Consequently, there doesn't seem to be any easy answer to the problem of corporate drug testing.

Although some people will quit using drugs in response to routine drug testing, it is unrealistic to assume that it will significantly reduce drug use in the general population. Most individuals who are seriously bent on using drugs are going to use them no matter how many tests are performed on them. Moreover, as long as there are going to be drug tests, there are going to be ways to get around them. Why even now there are already several nationally advertised methods for treating one's urine so that it comes out "clean" in a test. Abbie Hoffman's humorous book *Steal This Urine Test,* for example, offers dozens of ways of getting around drug testing.

To be fair, though, there is undoubtedly a small minority of recreational users who will unflinchingly give up their occasional habit in order to protect their security on the job. In these cases routine drug testing does seem to be a somewhat effective way of reducing drug usage in the work force. On the other hand, though, anyone who would quit their drug use overnight because of on-the-job-testing wouldn't be that serious of a user in the first place. Such a person would probably end up quitting on his own eventually if allowed to do so.

Clearly, drug testing misses the true issue at hand when it comes to having a genuine effect on the real inner reasons why people use drugs. For as long as people inwardly want to use drugs, no amount of external deterrence such as drug testing will get them to stop. To really make a difference in the extent of drug abuse in this country we must first reduce the user's inner motivation to use drugs. Accordingly, instead of spending millions upon millions of dollars chasing down smugglers and testing our work force, we should be using that money to help reduce many of the reasons why people use drugs in the first place, such as poverty, unemployment, poor life-style, and ignorance about the true effects of drug abuse.

Our government is wrong. The people of this country aren't blind sheep who only use drugs because they are available. They are individuals who consciously choose to use drugs either out of ignorance, boredom, or poverty-inspired despair. If our government leaders would just wake up and begin spending their billions on these fundamental causes of drug abuse, significant progress towards a drug-free America will finally take place.

10.1 What Parents Can Do

Parents are perhaps the single most important group of people in our society who can make a significant difference in the amount of drugs that are consumed by our children and teenagers. Sadly, though, many abusive parents actually cause their kids to use more drugs instead of less. It is for this reason that parents need to be actively involved in any serious effort to fight drug abuse in this country.

If you are a parent, the single most important thing you can do to help prevent your children from using drugs is to establish a loving relationship with them, for it is this loving relationship which will later give them the strength to say no to drugs. This means spending quality time with them every single day, if at all possible. It means listening to them and encouraging them to freely discuss their problems with you without fear of undue reprimand or punishment. To be sure, if your children love and respect you and sincerely regard you as their friend, they are MUCH less likely to let you down by using drugs.

On the other hand, if you constantly antagonize and oppose your children's best efforts, you are bound to make them hostile and resentful towards you. This is another vitally important rule to cast in stone: *Never antagonize your children to the point that they feel compelled to spite you.* On the contrary, guide them in the way they should go by being positive with them whenever possible; motivate them to do what you want by reinforcing them whenever they choose to behave in the desired direction. In behavioral psychology this pattern of selective reinforcement is known as shaping, and it can have an extremely powerful effect on producing the behavior you want if it is conducted properly.

Also, don't continually preach to your children in a negative fashion about the dangers of drug abuse, especially if you have a martini in one hand and a cigarette in the other. If you do, your children are likely to laugh all the way to the local drug dealer's house. And whatever you do, try to let your children know that you trust them; smelling their breath every time they come home will turn the house into a non-loving prison camp, and this will only give your children more reason to spite you.

In short, if you want to minimize the possibility of drug abuse in your children, do your very best to create a positive atmosphere at home. Remember: a house is not a home unless you specifically make it so. Therefore, do your best to make your children want to come home at night; do your best to make them want to talk to you openly and honestly about their personal problems. If you don't know how to do this, read up on the subject or seek some help from a professional psychologist; after all, that's what they're there for. If you do, you'll be glad you did; if you don't, you might easily turn out to be sorry for the rest of your life.

Chapter 11

CONCLUSION

Drug abuse has suddenly become the number one area of public concern in this country. Unfortunately, though, it has taken an almost prodigious amount of suffering to arouse this concern. But now that it has been aroused, it is time for us to show our concern by doing everything in our power to fight this dreaded scourge on our society.

We mustn't ever think that we are overreacting to this problem, because it is the very fabric of our society which is being seriously eroded by drug and alcohol abuse in this country. And let's face it, our society is comprised first and foremost of people; consequently, when our people become compromised by the abuse of drugs, our very nation becomes equally compromised, and this in turn can seriously jeapordize our continued sovereignty in the global community. Clearly, something radical needs to be done to combat this problem as soon as possible, otherwise our country could easily end up facing the same fate that the ancient Roman Empire had to suffer: a self-imposed decay into weakness through a gradual loss of control in the general population.

It is my sincere hope that this book will be of some help in our never-ending struggle to free ourselves from the chemical causes of addiction and slavery. Even if it only helps a single individual, all the effort that has gone into the writing of it will have been worthwhile.

In conclusion, it is imperative that we direct our very best efforts towards overcoming the curse of drug addiction in our society, since it is the very dignity and survivability of our humanity which is at stake. Indeed, it appears likely that the success we will have at combating this problem will mirror the success we will have as a nation in maintaining our respect and sovereignty in the global community.

INDEX